James Freeman Clarke

Essentials and non-essentials in Religion

James Freeman Clarke

Essentials and non-essentials in Religion

ISBN/EAN: 9783337079758

Printed in Europe, USA, Canada, Australia, Japan

Cover: Foto ©Lupo / pixelio.de

More available books at **www.hansebooks.com**

Essentials

and

Non-Essentials in Religion.

SIX LECTURES

DELIVERED IN THE MUSIC HALL, BOSTON,

BY

JAMES FREEMAN CLARKE,

AUTHOR OF "ORTHODOXY: ITS TRUTHS AND ERRORS," "STEPS OF BELIEF," "TEN GREAT RELIGIONS," "CHRISTIAN DOCTRINE OF PRAYER," "COMMON SENSE IN RELIGION," ETC.

BOSTON:
AMERICAN UNITARIAN ASSOCIATION,
7 TREMONT PLACE.
1878.

Copyright by
AMERICAN UNITARIAN ASSOCIATION.
1877.

Cambridge:
Press of John Wilson and Son.

These Six Lectures were delivered in the Music Hall, in Boston, this winter (1877), at the request of the American Unitarian Association; and, as they seem to have met the needs of many minds, are now published as they were delivered, with scarcely any alterations.

J. F. C.

BOSTON, *Dec.* 14, 1877.

I.
FAITH AND BELIEF. ESSENTIAL BELIEF CONCERNING GOD 1

II.
CHRIST AND CHRISTIANITY 33

III.
THE BIBLE 57

IV.
THE CHURCH AND WORSHIP 81

V.
CHRISTIAN EXPERIENCE 103

VI.
THE FUTURE LIFE 127

ESSENTIALS

AND

NON-ESSENTIALS IN RELIGION.

I.

THE DISTINCTION BETWEEN FAITH AND BELIEF.

I PROPOSE to speak of essentials and non-essentials in religion. My purpose is, not to defend a creed or a sect, but to point out that common ground of essential religion on which all good men can stand side by side. For it is mostly about non-essentials that men differ: on what is most vital or important, they usually agree. If, therefore, I can show the essential unity of faith, or life, which underlies all seeming opposition and contradiction of sects or creeds, I shall do a more important work than by making the most triumphant argument in favor of my own opinions, or against those of other sects or parties.

I therefore intend to show what are the essentials and what the non-essentials in the faith of the Christian church concerning God, Christ, the Bible, the Church, Christian experience, and the Future Life.

I know that, to many, all such attempts seem hazardous. Religion is so important a matter that they cannot believe any thing belonging to it to be unessential. The Holy Spirit sanctifies to their minds every sacrament of their church, every word of their liturgy, every part of their creed, every sentence in their Bible. It seems to them sacrilege to say or to hint that any of these great helps to religion are not essential to it. If not the very citadel, they are at least outworks to be defended to the last, as a necessary protection to the citadel.

The inevitable result of this is division and strife in the church. To each sect and party its own special forms of faith and worship seem not only useful, but vital: it is dangerous to permit any other. The Episcopalian thinks that without bishops there is no church; the Presbyterian clings to every chapter and section of the Assembly's Catechism; the Baptist cannot take the Lord's Supper with the most saintly Christian who has not been immersed. There can be but one truth, one Lord, one faith, one baptism, say they, and that is ours. We honestly believe that we are right, and therefore we must believe others to be wrong. Can two walk together unless they are agreed?

Paul said of himself and his fellow-Christians, "We have this treasure in earthen vessels;" but to the majority of Christian believers now, the vessel which contains their faith is as important as the faith itself. Because I drink the water of salvation out of a Unitarian glass instead of a Methodist cup or an Episcopal vase, it is thought that I cannot be partaking of the water of life.

Nearly twenty-five centuries ago, Æsop told the story of the twigs which could not be broken when united together, but were easily snapped when separated. The Christian church, in its numerous divisions, still illustrates the sad moral of that fable. Here, in Boston, we have one hundred and eighty Protestant churches, but they are divided into eight or ten different sects, which work entirely independently of each other. Suppose they should form one grand union for Christian work, to attack the evils around us. What an immense influence for good might these one hundred and eighty churches exercise, if they co-operated against the evils of pauperism, intemperance, licentiousness, ignorance, and crime! Suppose they had one central building, to which delegates from these churches should come to consider and act as one body in making Boston more pure, sweet, and safe. The Baptists might still immerse; the Episcopalians keep their bishops and liturgy, — but, being thus united in one body against practical evils, how sure and soon might not God's Kingdom come among us!

The difficulty in the way of this consummation is that the church still confounds essentials and non-essentials. There being confessedly but one end, one thing needful, as the object of all religion, they suppose that there can be but one true and right way to that end; though Paul has taught that there are differences of administration, but one Lord, and diversities of operation, but one God.

A great city, like New York or Chicago, has but one purpose, — the bringing together of those within and those without for mutual advantage. But each city has numerous avenues by which it is entered. There are roads which concentrate toward it from all quarters. There are numerous lines of railroads, which bring to it long trains of passengers and freight, entering the city on all sides; steamers come to it by the lake, the river, the sea. But we imagine that the vast city of God, the heavenly Jerusalem, has only one entrance, and that, the turnpike, where we collect the toll.

The Lord has made his children very different from each other, and, being thus different, he has provided many different ways by which they shall come to him.

Other and very great evils arise from this want of religious perspective which confounds the spirit with the letter, the substance with the form, the permanent with the transient, the kernel with the shell, the soul with the body. The spirit and substance of religion are one and eternal; the same yesterday, to-day, and for ever. The form changes, the body decays and dies, the kernel in its growth shatters its shell. The law of change applies to the body of religion, as to that of all other human interests. If religion in its spirit is divine and eternal, in its body it is human and changing. Every church form, ritual, sacrament, is human, therefore temporary. Every church-creed is elaborated by the wit of man, therefore none can last for ever. The Christian church must say, as the Apostle Paul said, "When I was a child, I spake as a child, I understood as a child, I thought as a child; but, when I became a man, I put away childish things." This great apostle, possessing one of the most majestic of human intellects, declared that his own creed, precious as it was to him, was to pass away, and be forgotten. "I know in part," said he; "and I teach in part. But, when that which is perfect is come, then that which is in part shall be done away. For now we see, as in a mirror, darkly [referring to the metallic mirrors of his time], but then face to face." The light of the intellect is reflected light, therefore we call it reflection; hereafter it will be intuition. From the accuracy of each man's thought, even the wisest, there are to be made three deductions: we must first correct it for the human equation, since all belief is relative; then we must correct it again for the personal equation, since each man's idiosyncrasy colors his thought; and finally we must correct it for the aberration produced by progress and development. It was a great discovery in astronomy, when Bradley found that the progress of the earth through space caused an aberration of the light coming from the stars, and that this aberration must be allowed for. So we must allow for the aberration of light in our own minds, caused by the fact that we are in progress. The individual, as he grows, puts away childish things; and so society and humanity, moving swiftly forward in the vast orbit of its heaven-ordained progress through the ages and eternities, must also put away its childish things, and for ever be learning more and more the language of manly thought and manly piety.

The soul which has no singleness of aim is distracted and divided, and loses its power. If the eye is single, the whole body is full of light; if the eye is double, the whole body is full of darkness. It is so in every thing else. It is so also in religion. The superstition which makes secondary things of equal importance with the primary clouds and degrades the soul. When Jesus came to the house of the Jewish maidens and saw Martha's mind distracted with a thousand cares, while Mary, recognizing what was *then* of supreme importance, used this great opportunity by devoting herself solely to listening to the divine truth which had entered her home, Jesus saw in it the images of dissipation and of singleness of soul. "Martha,

Martha, thou art careful and troubled about many things; but one thing is needful." The church has always had its many Marthas and its few Marys, — its Marthas, careful and troubled about creeds and rituals, sacraments and sabbaths, priesthood and altar; and its Marys, not indeed wishing that these should be left undone, but never letting them interfere with the one thing needful, — love to God and love to man.

To all this what do the Marthas reply? What did the original Martha reply to Jesus? Probably she said, "It is all very well for Mary to be neglecting her duties, in order to listen to you; but who is to help me get the dinner?" So the Marthas in the church reply: "It is all very well to say that love is the one thing needful; that love fulfils the whole law; that he who dwells in love dwells in God, and God in him. But how are we to get that love, except we use the means? He who wishes the end wishes the means? Piety and charity are, we admit, the only essential ends; but the means are equally essential. It is essential, in order to have love, to be in the true church; for out of this there is no salvation. It is essential to have the true belief, for we are saved by the word of truth, and without faith no man can be justified. It is necessary also to be converted; for unless a man is born again, he cannot see the kingdom of God.

In future lectures, I shall discuss the essentials and the non-essentials in regard to the church and conversion. I now ask you to attend to this second point made by our friends. the Christian Marthas. They speak thus: "The New Testament says we are justified by faith. When the Apostle was called upon by the jailer to tell him what he must do to be saved, he did not reply, 'Love God and man,' but he said, 'Believe on the Lord Jesus Christ, and thou shalt be saved.' And Paul was right, for that was the step he could take at once, and by an immediate act of obedience accept Christ as his Saviour; then, having done that, he would reach at last the end, which is love. Love, therefore, is the essential end; but a true faith is the no less essential means to that end." This is their argument.

If this be true, and if a true faith means a correct belief of the great doctrines of Christianity, then it follows that the one thing needful for us is, first of all, to study theology, in order to find out what the true and vital doctrines are. We ought carefully to read the innumerable controversies about the Trinity, Total Depravity, the Atonement, the Deity of Christ, and the Way of Salvation. Until this is done, and done correctly, and the true belief is reached, there is no safety. How much mental misery, anxiety, gloom, despair, have come from this doctrine that a sound belief on such points as these is essential to the salvation of the soul! Moreover, the moment you assume that any accurate statement of belief is essential, you can find no place where you can logically stop. For in any system of doctrine every part is logically dependent on every other part, and the whole must stand or fall together. As an illustration of this, let me state a fact from ecclesiastical history. The Presbyterian church of the United States has a creed, and that creed is the Assembly's Catechism. Now, parts of that statement are so behind and below the convictions reached by modern thought that it has been held very loosely in many places, and accepted merely for substance of doctrine. In the year 1837, an earnest theologian, Robert J. Breckinridge, induced the General Assembly to excommunicate four synods, containing some forty thousand members, for heresy; the error being in relation to the origin of sin. The belief of the Old School was this: that God could have prevented sin, but would not do it, because it was essential to a moral system. The error of the New School, for which the synods were excommunicated, was in believing that God would have prevented sin, but could not, because it was essential to a moral system. Now this distinction seems to us a small matter; but a trained theologian sees that it is essential to the integrity of the whole system that the "could" should precede the "would" in this statement. So, when a single leading proposition of a creed is made essential, every minute inference becomes also essential. A creed is like a chain, whose strength is measured by the strength of the weakest part. An acute theologian is like a skilled engineer building a dam, who knows that, if he leaves the smallest leak in any part, the whole dam will be finally swept away.

What, then, is our reply to this argument? We admit that faith is an essential element of human progress, — essential as a means to the growth and perfection of man. But we deny that belief is the same as faith, and we deny that the belief of any proposition is essential to human salvation. We fully agree with John Wesley, who once said that "a string of opinions is no more Christian faith than a string of beads is Christian practice."

When the jailer at Philippi believed on the Lord Jesus Christ, what was his theological belief? What were his opinions about the Trinity or the Atonement? His faith was simply a trust in the superior power and goodness of that being of whom these wonderful persons before him declared themselves the messengers. The servant, he thought, could not be greater than the master; nor he that was sent greater than he that sent him. Therefore, he was willing to trust to this new advent of light and power, and joins this persecuted body whose souls were so full of calm and joy, and who seemed so protected by a present Providence. His faith was trust in something higher and better than himself.

What was the theological belief of those whom Jesus healed? What was the creed of the sinful woman whom he forgave, and to whom he said, "Thy faith hath saved thee; go in peace"? What were the doctrinal opinions of the Roman soldier, of whom he declared, "I have not found so great faith, no, not in Israel"? What were the speculative dogmas held by all those whose faith is commemorated in the eleventh chapter of the Hebrews? What were the views of Abel, in regard to the Trinity? Was Enoch a Calvinist or an Arminian? What doctrines were held by Noah and Abraham and Sarah. Isaac. Jacob, Gideon, Barak, and Samson? In all these cases, what was their faith but this: a looking up with trust to something higher than themselves; better than themselves; something above this visible and sensible world; a confidence that. besides all that is seen and temporal. there is something divine, invisible, eternal? This was their faith, and this is the substance of all faith. For this their faith, Samson and Gideon are commended as examples to us all.

This faith we believe and know to be essential to progress. We can only rise to a higher plane by trusting in some power better than ourselves. In order to go up. we must look up.

God gives, in the morning of life, a great provision of faith as an outfit. Little children are full of trust, and by this trust they learn rapidly. Because men and women are larger and stronger than themselves. they naturally look upon them as knowing every thing and able to do every thing. They may often be deceived and misled by their infantile credulity; but without it they could never make such rapid progress. Undeterred either by vanity or doubt, they ask a thousand questions every day of every one about them. This perpetual looking up for guidance, knowledge, help, is what makes the soul of a child unfold, as the buds open in the warm airs of spring.

As children grow up, they do not outgrow the need of perpetual faith in their fellow-men. The more highly civilized society becomes, the more men are obliged to trust in each other. Savage life is filled with distrust and suspicion. The backwoodsman trusts in himself, and depends on himself to supply his own wants. But as society is developed through its different stages, from the savage state to that of the hunter, from the hunter's life to the pastoral state, from that to the highly complex condition of modern society in Christian lands, mutual trust increases. We sleep in peace, trusting to the protection of the police. We go to our affairs, trusting our homes to the guardianship of the laws. We trust in the merchant to sell us the article we need; to our physician to understand and treat aright our illness; to our lawyer to defend our rights when assailed. All our society is built on the perpetual faith of man in man. We walk by faith all day long. True, there is deception, knavery, cheating; but society would stand still to-morrow if there were not a hundred times as much truth as falsehood in the transactions of common life. When we trust our brother, whom we have seen, we are learning to trust God, whom we have not seen. Our faith in man is really faith in the great laws of human nature: it is faith that humanity is essentially good, not evil, made by God and a manifestation of him.

The difference between faith and belief is obvious, and the distinction very important. Belief is purely an intellectual act, the result of argument and evidence. Where the evidence is before us, belief is involuntary. The object of belief is a proposition, and there are no degrees about it. We either believe the proposition or we do not. If we hesitate about it, and are not quite ready to assent to it, then we do not yet believe it. And a belief does not necessarily make a man any better. The devils believe and tremble. You find good men and bad men believing all sorts of creeds. Some men are uninfluenced by the noblest creeds, though they assent to them; some are uninjured by the lowest and basest.

In all these respects, how different is faith! This involves an intellectual element indeed, for we trust in some power or person whom we know. He that cometh to God or to man must believe that they are. But faith has also a moral element, for we trust in good, not in evil. Hope is also involved in it. We have faith in something better than we yet see. Love is in it, for we do not give our faith except where we also give something of our affection. And, moreover, faith is an act. We give ourselves in trust, we lean, we confide, we repose on the good which we know and to which we look up. And this faith, like all other acts, increases and strengthens by habit. We can have a little faith, and we can acquire more. And this trust in something higher, better, nobler, wiser, always makes us better ourselves. By looking up, we rise. And thus we realize the truth of those lines of Daniel which Coleridge was so fond of quoting: —

> "Unless above himself he can
> Erect himself, how poor a thing is man!"

Individual man is weak, ignorant, liable to deceive and be deceived. But the human nature of which he partakes is higher than he, — better than any individual, — for it is that common human nature which contains the law of progress, and the power of an endless development upward and onward. Our faith in man is therefore still the same. It is looking up to something higher. It is trust in man not only as he is, but as he is made and meant to be. It is the substance of things hoped for, the evidence of things not seen.

But the most wonderful fact of human nature remains to be stated. It is man's religious nature and his religious faith.

Wherever man exists, he believes in God. His belief may be of a low and rudimentary kind, but it is there. A creature of time and sense, surrounded with the engrossing interests of this life, this life never satisfies him. He looks out of the seen into the unseen, looks up out of the sunlight of this sensible world into the mystery of the all-surrounding world outside of space and time.

> "Placed on this isthmus of a middle state,
> A being darkly wise and rudely great;
> Chaos of thought and passion all confused;
> Still by himself abused, or disabused;
> Created half to rise and half to fall,
> Great Lord of all things, yet a prey to all;
> Sole judge of truth, in endless error hurled,
> The glory, jest, and riddle of the world."

Yes, man is all that, but something more. Some convictions, some ideas, deep rooted in his inmost nature, hold him fast to the infinite and eternal. He looks back through the long geologic ages, but they cannot content his reason: he finds an eternity behind them all. He looks through the immensities of the universe to the faint star-clusters at frightful distances in the enormous space which surrounds our little globe, and his reason commands him to believe in an infinite space beyond. He looks up, in imagination, through a long vista of intelligences higher than man, angels and archangels, cherubim and seraphim. Analogy teaches him to believe that higher than thought can climb, or the fancy conceive, or the understanding comprehend, there must be series above series, rank above rank of powers; a hierarchy of spiritual beings extending without end up to the throne of God. But he cannot rest in this conception: he must go beyond, and gaze on the one great central power of the universe, — above all height, below all depth, — the Almighty, the Eternal, the One above. He is so made that he can never stop in any lower worship, but passes up through all mythologies of old religion to the First Cause, the perfect Being.

This is the natural faith of man, not of one sect or creed; and the primal faith, which Jesus came to restore and to exalt. Abraham saw his day, because Abraham believed essentially in the truth of Jesus. Something of his day was also seen by Socrates, by Zoroaster, by Confucius, by Buddha, for they also lifted their race to a higher faith in some unspoken majesty of truth and goodness; some radiance seen, though but in a glass darkly, of the holy spirit of truth. This faith, at least, they all had in an unseen Power, higher than any thing seen, who would help those who came to Him.

I am a transcendentalist. I do not believe that man's senses tell him all he knows. Man is more certain of those truths which come to him through his reason than of those which come through his senses. "All his knowledge," according to the statement of Immanuel Kant, "all his knowledge begins *with* sensible experience, but all does not come *from* experience." He knows the ideal realities received through reason better than he knows those transmitted through sense. He knows cause and effect, phenomenon and substance, right and wrong, the infinite and the eternal, his own identity, his power of free choice.

These ideas are divinely created within him, divinely rooted in the very texture of his reason. By the unalterable and majestic laws of nature, which pervade the world, unchanging and persistent, God has bound the outward universe to himself, and established all its variety into one vast order. And by the ideas, equally fixed and unchanging, in the soul of man, he holds fast to himself every created intelligence in a similar unity, and is the centre of the visible and invisible universe.

To this statement, however, I hear this reply: "This may be all true, as far as it goes. This is pure theism, and is no doubt a vast step upward from sheer unbelief. But it is not Christian faith. That is more than a mere instinct of trust in God: it is trust in him, because of what he has done for us through his Son. It is trust in God's grace, mediated through the sacrifice of Christ."

I gladly admit and proclaim that Christ has lifted the world to a higher faith than it had before, or has now outside of Christianity. But is it *a different* faith? or is it not *the same*, deepened, purified, and elevated? When Paul spoke to the Greeks at Athens, he did not tell them he had brought them another God or a new religion; but that he had come to make clear to them the being whom they already worshipped. "Whom ye ignorantly worship, him declare I unto you." If Paul believed that the Greeks were ignorantly worshipping the true God, why should we deny that the Chinese and Hindoos, the ancient Persians and Egyptians, the negroes of Africa and the Indians of North America, have also been ignorantly worshipping the true God? Have not they also, in all their different idolatries and superstitions, been feeling after God, if haply they might find him? When the Indian mother, whose infant had fallen into the river, stretched out her arms and cried, "O Thou Great Everywhere! save my child!" was she not crying out to the living God, as David was when he fasted and prayed for *his* child, as any Christian mother is who calls on God to-day?

To see what is the essential element in Christian faith, let us analyze it, as we find it developed in Christian experience. For this purpose we will select some of the most perfect specimens, the highest types in the history of our religion.

In the fourth century of our era, there lived a man whose influence on human thought has been so vast, so continued, so unbroken, that it fills us with astonishment at the power sometimes delegated to a single man. The theology of Europe has been moulded during fourteen centuries by this master-mind. He was one of those

> "Fiery souls, which, working out their way,
> Fretted the puny body to decay,
> And o'er-informed their tenement of clay."

There is not a little Baptist church to-day in Kansas, not a Methodist church in Florida, not a Scotch farmer or English statesman, but is influenced by that African bishop. Not a Roman Catholic missionary in Japan and Brazil but is guided by the dead hand of Aurelius Augustine. His theology we know, and we reject it. But what was his *faith*? Read his "Confessions," and see. In that book, he has unlocked his heart. There is the deepest, sweetest essence of his religion. And, changing possibly a few words or phrases, there is not a sentence, not a line of that most devout of all appeals to God, but could be uttered as the prayer of a Unitarian Christian, and meet the deepest wants of a Buddhist and Lama in the mountains of Thibet. It is a cry of the child to his father and mother; a simple utterance of perfect trust in an infinite love; it is human love casting itself on the infinite tenderness, with perfect confidence that he hears and that he pities.

And now come down twelve centuries later. The Roman Catholics regard Augustine as the Father of their theology. Let us take the founder of Protestantism, Martin Luther. The battle-cry by which this hero broke the sleep of ages was the echo of Paul's words, "We are justified by faith." What led Luther to his great work? His own profound experience. A poor monk in an Augustinian monastery, he tried to save his soul by prayer and fasting, penance and sacrament. But all in vain: these monkish practices only made him feel more heavily the burden of his sins. At last, by the mediation of a brother monk, Luther was led to go to God himself, and find a Saviour in him. God, in Christ, reconciled Luther to himself. Henceforth all the ceremonies and sacraments of the church, all acts of ascetic denial, all hope of salvation by priestly absolution or papal indulgence, were cast aside. Simple faith in God, through Christ, had created a joy in Luther's heart. a sense of heavenly peace and hope, that was like a new moral force sent into the world. It shook the seat of the papacy in Rome; it penetrated the emperor's palace and the peasant's hut. Pardon freely bestowed, unbought grace and goodness, — this was the living experience which made a new world and a new civilization in Europe. Compare Luther's faith with that of Augustine, and you will find them essentially the same. Their views of church and of life were a thousand miles apart: their faith was the same simple trust in the divine love.

One more example from later times. During the last century there arose in England a religious movement, which, to my mind, combines in itself more depth and breadth, more freedom and more elevation than any other since that of Luther. And the root of this was another return to the same simple element of childlike trust in God. When John Wesley was crossing the Atlantic on his way to Georgia, to become a missionary to the heathen, he was what we now call a Ritualist, or Puseyite, in religion. The method of salvation to him was to fast and pray, to renounce the world, to save his soul by fidelity to all the minutest requisitions of the church, by daily communion, hours of prayer, and the like. But on this voyage they encountered a fearful gale ; and in the confusion and terror of the storm, when the awful tempest laid the vessel on its beam, and they seemed about to perish, some Moravians on board were calmly singing hymns of trust to God. The honest Wesley, looking into his own heart, found no such tranquillity there, but a secret, unconquered fear of death and judgment. After the gale had blown out, he asked the Moravians why they felt no fear. They replied, "We trust in God." "But your women and your children, they also were so calm," said Wesley. "Our women and children are not afraid to die; they also trust in God." Here was a mystery to Wesley. He had believed in all the orthodoxy of the church; had practised all the ceremonies of his religion more than others; had been accounted a man of the most eminent piety. What was this faith, then, that he needed? This idea haunted him during his stay in Georgia, and gave him no rest. It sent him back to England. There he took no counsel with bishops or doctors, or those called leaders of the church, but found his poor Moravian friends to learn their secret. At last, after many struggles and prayers, he learned the truth, that

> "A man's best things are nearest him,
> Lie close around his feet."

The living faith, which he had missed so long in

his arduous struggle for salvation, was the faith of a little child, who knows nothing about sin or salvation, but trusts without a doubt in a Father's love. It was because it was so simple that he had missed it so long. He had looked for a salvation strange, mysterious, and difficult, to be bought by sacrifice and worship, and the solemn forms of an ancient church. But it was simply and only to forget about himself and his salvation, to leave penance and prayers, and to put himself into the arms of the heavenly Father, thinking no more about himself or his own soul, but about saving the souls of others in the strength of the Infinite love. Thus Wesley passed through exactly the same experience as that of Paul, Augustine, and Luther, and arrived at last at the same essential faith, and found the truth of Christ's great saying, that to be converted was only to become again as a little child. Then was revealed to him the meaning which our translation misses, of that other profound saying of the Master: "He who would save his soul loses it; but he who is willing to lose his soul for the sake of the gospel love and work, he finds it." Not when we think about saving our soul can we save it; but when we think about God's love and his children's needs, then it is saved for us, while we are caring for others. In that hour, Wesley passed up out of the religion of ritualism to a higher plane. In that hour, and not before, was Methodism born. Then, through this new experience of Wesley, was a fresh impulse of heavenly love poured into human hearts, and a vast movement began which has brought blessings to millions on both sides of the Atlantic.

Thus, in all these cases, we see that faith is essentially the same thing. It is casting all our care for body and soul on Him who cares for us. It is trusting in God as a faithful Creator, in Christ as a dear friend and helper, who teaches us to say, "Our Father." Many theologies, but one faith. There may be a hundred beliefs, as there may be a hundred roads to London or New York. But, when we have entered the city, we are all in the same place, side by side. There is neither Jew nor Greek, neither Trinitarian nor Unitarian there; neither Catholic nor Protestant, but all are one in Christ Jesus, and in the love of the great Father.

Faith may even sometimes appear under what seems to be unbelief. A soldier, dying on a field of battle in our war for freedom and union, was asked by a chaplain, who tells the story, to trust in the atoning blood of Christ, and ask God for pardon. "No. not now," said the soldier: "I did not do it when I was strong and well: I will not do it now merely to please God and to prevent him from sending me to hell. That would be the act of a coward." Though the chaplain did not see it, this was really an act of trust in God. The soldier preferred rather to trust himself to God as he was than try to pacify the Almighty by a death-bed confession. And that was faith. So when John Stuart Mill wrote his famous sentence, protesting against the notion of Mr. Mansell that the goodness of God could be essentially different from ours, and declared that "if he must go to hell for believing in the goodness which seemed to *him* good, then to hell he would go," he also was really expressing faith in God as a faithful Creator, who, having made the human mind to believe in right and in truth, would not demand of it to believe differently. And this saying of Mill's is also in essence one with the doctrine of those New England divines who thought no man truly converted till he was willing to be damned for the glory of God. For John Stuart Mill said that he was ready to be damned for the cause of honesty and truth, and that *is* for the glory of God, so far as any thing we do can glorify him. Being honest, being true, standing by our true convictions, that glorifies God. The old Arab sheik, Job, said the same when he refused to confess himself a sinner until he could see how and why he was a sinner, and answered the pious persuasions of his friends with this immortal utterance: "Shall I speak *words of wind* to the Almighty? Can I please *him*, as I would please a man, by outward submission and empty flattery?"

The same thought is expressed in another way in one of the poems of our New England Robert Burns. It is the same essential, universal faith, which, beginning low down in the heart of the savage and the Pagan, unfolds into higher forms in the Christian, but is always the same in Catholic or Protestant, Methodist or Unitarian. And so we find it expressed in the tender strain of our Quaker poet, who says, as Jesus said in the garden, and as all true faith responds everywhere, "Not my will, but thine, be done:"—

> "The autumn-time has come
> On woods that dream of bloom,
> And over purpling vines
> The low sun fainter shines.

"The aster-flower is failing,
  The hazel's gold is paling;
  Yet overhead, more near,
  The eternal stars appear.

" And present gratitude
  Insures the future's good;
  And for the things I see
  I trust the things to be,

"That, in the paths untrod
  And the long days of God,
  My feet shall still be led,
  My heart be comforted.

"Others shall sing the song,
  Others shall right the wrong,
  Finish what I begin,
  And all I fail of, win.

" What matter, I or they?
  Mine, or another's day,
  So the right word be said,
  And life be sweeter made?

" Hail to the coming singers!
  Hail to the brave light-bringers!
  Forward I reach, and share
  All that they sing, or dare.

" The airs of heaven blow o'er me,
  A glory shines before me,
  Of what mankind shall be,
  Pure, generous, brave, and free.

> "Ring, bells, in unreared steeples,
> The joy of new-born peoples!
> Sound, trumpets, far-off blown.
> Your triumph is my own."

This is the very breath and essence of that faith which trusts the great God, the Divine Friend, the Infinite Tenderness, the dear Father of us all; above, below, around, within; from whom, and through whom, and to whom are all things.

II.

CHRIST AND CHRISTIANITY.

THE two views on this subject which are the most significant, influential, and interesting, stand as opposite extremes. First comes the grand orthodoxy of the Church, which declares Christianity to have been a miraculous interposition of the Supreme Being for the rescue of the human race; declares that Christianity is the only true religion, out of which there is no possible salvation; that Christ was very God and very Man, — Prophet, Priest, and King. Prophet, as teaching infallibly supernatural truth. Priest, as dying to make an atonement to God for the sins of the human race. King, as God himself, second person in the Trinity, whose right it is to demand absolute obedience from all his creatures.

This view stands at one end of the scale of religious belief. We will call it SUPERNATURALISM. At the other end of the scale is the view of those who deny any supernatural character to Christ or Christianity, — the view of such writers as Strauss in Germany, Rénan in France, Conway in England, Frothingham in America. According to them, Christianity was a natural development of humanity, like every other religion; better in some things than they, — good and useful once, but now outgrown, discredited, and passed by. Instead of it we are to have either *no* religion, but instead thereof science, art, and literature, — or else a larger and better religion, that of Humanity. We will call this view NATURALISM.

Now, when we find two such opposite and extreme views, each advocated by earnest and intelligent men, honest in their convictions, and bent on converting the whole world to their own faith; where, probably, does the truth lie?

The old answer was, "The truth lies somewhere between these extremes, somewhere in the middle. Believe a little less than supernaturalism, believe a little more than naturalism, and you will be about right." But half views are feeble views. At each extreme there is an idea, a principle, and therefore strong conviction; in the middle there is apt to be only confusion of thought and weakness of purpose. A better philosophy of the human mind has taught us that truth is not in the middle, but on both sides; that one extreme embodies one truth, and the other embodies its antagonistic truth. On either side is conviction; in the middle, hesitation and lukewarmness. Goethe long ago expressed this view: "You think that truth is in the mean between extremes; truth is not there, but the paradox." What truth, let us therefore ask, is there in the old supernaturalism, and what truth in the modern naturalism? Finding and accepting the truths on both sides, they will supply each other's defects, correct each other's errors, sift out non-essentials, and leave the essentials. This is the method of modern science, — to find all the truth there is, sure that it will all be found at last to be in harmony with itself.

What is the truth in supernaturalism?

It is that Christianity is not only deeper, higher, broader, better than any other religion, but essentially different from every other, in this: that its truth is so absolute and so universal as to be fitted to become the religion of mankind. It is capable of doing all the work which can be asked of a religion; that is, to teach ever essential truth, to give to man peace with God, and to purify him from evil. To prove Christianity to be a supernatural religion is not necessary; neither is this

an adequate distinction. For God, who is above
nature, is always descending into nature, so that
the supernatural is in all things. God, as Paul
declares, "is above all, and through all, and in
you all." To say that Christianity is supernatural is to say, not too much, but too little.
Nor is it enough to say, "Christianity is the
exclusively true religion." We must go further,
and maintain that it is the *inclusively* true religion.
That which excludes and shuts out is not so great
as that which takes in and receives. So Christianity has received into itself all the good of many
systems, — the philosophy and art of Greece, the
laws of Rome, the mysticism of India, the monotheism of the Jews, the triad of Egypt, the war
between good and evil taught by Zoroaster, the
reverence for ancestors and the conservatism of
China, the Scandinavian faith in liberty and
progress. All the prophets who have been since
the world began, and all the civilizations of the
past, have, like the wise men of the East, brought
their gifts to the infant Messiah. There is in this
wonderful religion the power of assimilating to
itself all that is true and good everywhere. It is
like the sea, "into which all rivers run, and yet
it is not full."

The only progressive religion in the world to-day is Christianity. All others are decayed, arrested, or retrograde. But Christianity is capable of self-development. It unfolds itself into new forms, puts forth new branches, and makes every day a new heavens and a new earth. In ages of universal war, it unfolded into monastic institutions, — islands of peace in the midst of the stormy ocean; oases of knowledge in the desert of ignorance. When all society seemed falling apart amid the deluge of barbarism, it created the Papacy, as a central force to hold Christendom together. When this force became excessive and tyrannical, it suddenly produced the Protestant Reformation, which saved personal liberty in Europe. And when this outbreak of fiery lava had become too rigid, it again burst forth in such fountains of thought as Puritanism, Presbyterianism, Quakerism, Methodism, and the multiform varieties of modern opinion.

I am told that Christianity stands in the way of progress; that it is an incubus on human thought. Explain then, if you can, the manifest fact that the progress of humanity in science, art, literature, is co-extensive with Christendom. Who goes to-day to study in Mohammedan universities?

What astronomical discoveries are made in the observatories of China? Was it a Hindu who invented the steam engine, the locomotive, the photograph, the electric telegraph? Who are the great painters and sculptors of Turkey, Russia, Japan? Mention, if you please, the poets, historians, mathematicians, orators, novelists, philosophers among the Buddhists. In Christendom alone is the human race in progress, and it is the only religion which is itself progressive. We have a right to claim that it will become more and more the light of the world.

The principle of this wonderful vitality is to be found in Christ himself. Christianity is not an abstract creed, a system of thought; it is not a philosophical system, — it is the personal influence of a great soul. Christendom may say, as the Apostle said, "The life I now live, I live by faith in the Son of God." One method by which the Creator causes the progress of humanity is by sending new impulses into the world through great men. Every civilization has been largely made what it is by the influence of great souls. Greece became Greece by means of Aristides and Miltiades, Socrates and Plato; Aristotle, Homer, Æschylus, Pindar, Thucydides, Phidias. Take the great men out of European history, — its goodly company of heroes and saints, its noble army of prophets, poets, and statesmen, — and it would collapse to the dead level of Africa. What would England be without its Shakespeare and Spenser; its Locke, Newton, Milton; its Alfred, and Cromwell, and Hampden? What would America be if we had never had the Pilgrim Fathers, nor Samuel Adams, nor Washington, nor Franklin?

> These are the living lights,
> That from our bold green heights
>   Shall shine afar,
> Till those who name the name
> Of freedom, to the flame
> Come, as the Magi came
>   To Bethlehem's star.

The great souls of history almost constitute history. But *one* towers above them all, — so that, as Horace said of Zeus, "There is nothing like him, nothing next to him." When we think of China, we name Confucius. Zoroaster shines through the darkness of three thousand years from ancient Bactria. The mild Buddha has spread his benign influence over the whole of Eastern Asia during twenty-five centuries. The civilizations of which these were the inspiration are fading away; but wherever the word of Jesus goes to-day, new life flows from it into the soul. Liberty of speech and thought grows out of it; popular education attends it; a government of laws, not force, has been created by it. It balances order against freedom; it combines conservatism and reform; it brings consolation to the bereaved, comfort to the sorrowing, and help to the forlorn. And all this is simply an unfolding of the life of Christ himself.

I have seen on the outskirts of our land a town spring up, like Jacob's gourd, almost in a night. I have been in such places where there might be a population of perhaps one or two thousand people, many of them outlaws and desperadoes, all of them unrestrained by the civilities of life. There were no laws there but such as the population chose to fancy; no churches, no schools, no newspapers; but bar-rooms and gambling-houses, fighting and profanity, and the mastery of the red-handed murderer. Into such a place as I have described, there comes some poor Methodist or Baptist preacher, all his worldly goods in his saddle-bags. He preaches where he can, — in a bar-room or a tavern, or perhaps in the street. He goes in the strength of God among these moral maniacs, and appeals to motives latent in their breasts and unknown to themselves. But conscience is roused; the sense of an awe and mystery higher than this world enters their souls. They awaken as from a horrid dream; they come to themselves, change their lives, and find a strange peace descending into their hearts. Our philosophers who write in their quiet studies in New York or Boston may believe that Christianity is outgrown, and that the splendid figure of Jesus has passed out of our philosophy. But while thousands of humble Christian preachers are thus, by the power of the divine word and life, laying the foundation of order in the land, I think that Christ is as near and as real to us to-day as he was to the Apostle Paul or the Apostle John.

I believe, with Augustine, with Luther, and with Fénélon, with Wesley and Swedenborg, that Christianity is the life of Jesus himself, prolonged and unfolded on the earth. We are told by modern critics that we cannot know much about the historic Christ, — there are so many contradictions and difficulties in the gospel narrative, and no harmonious whole. So speaks the lower criticism, analytic, destructive, negative. But the higher criticism, sympathetic, synthetic, positive, creative, ever brings the historic Christ more near to our understandings, no less than to our hearts. As the world obeys him more faithfully, it learns to know him more truly. When he went up to God. he did not go away from man. He is still the great power in human history, the great motor in human progress. He is still "the Word made flesh, dwelling among us."

And who was Christ? I do not accept the scholastic theology of the Church, the definitions of Aquinas, the phrases invented by Tertullian, because I think these formulas hide his real divinity. I believe him *more* divine than the Church has stated him to be, not less. I see in him *more* of God. not less, than I can find in this technical theology. These mediæval phrases do not reveal Christ; they conceal him. I lose, when I listen to them, my all-loving Father and my most tender of brothers. My mind is confused and darkened, not enlightened.

Leaving, then, all theological terms, and endeavoring to find the secret of this wonderful virtue, which has gone out of Jesus into the world, we ask what Jesus claimed to be, and what the New Testament teaches concerning him. We assume that however much the four Gospels may differ in details, in spirit and substance they are agreed. Admit all that the minute critics may claim, there is no doubt that these four honest and simple narratives present a portrait so original that they could not have invented it; so consistent with itself that it proves a real person behind it; and so superior to all that the world has seen that this person is an adequate explanation of the origin of that sublime faith which we call Christianity.

First. Then, whatever else he was, he is described as a perfect man. "made in all points like his brethren," tempted like a man, suffering like a man, calling all men his brother-men, praying to God like a man, and, at last, dying like a man. Instead of beginning with his divinity, as is the custom, and going down, we will begin with his humanity, and see how far we can go up.

Secondly. He was by birth a Jew, — a patriot, loving his country, his people, and its city, reverencing Moses and the prophets, and saying that he did not come to destroy them. But yet he was wholly emancipated from Jewish prejudices, bigotry, and narrowness; he was a radical in his treatment of the Jewish Sabbath, the Jewish temple, ritual, and priesthood. The worship he taught was not Jewish, but the worship of the Father in spirit and in truth. The honest publican he counted nearer to God than the pious Pharisee. And, in his description of the great judgment, he declared that not those who prophesied in his name, but those who did acts of righteousness and mercy, should enter into the kingdom of his Father. His religion was not Jewish, but human, and the title he loved best was the *Son of man*,— the man of men,— the one in whom humanity fully appears.

Thirdly. He calls himself "the Way, the Truth, and the Life;" he says, "For this end was I born, and for this cause came I into the world,— to bear witness to the truth." He bears witness to what he has seen of the Divine laws, — to what he not only thinks or believes, but knows. We can therefore rely on his authority, for it is the authority of insight and knowledge. He speaks what he knows, and testifies to what he has seen. He saw, with the inward eye of inspiration, the facts and laws of the spiritual world, as we see with the outward eye the facts of the physical world. He could no more be mistaken about the one than we can be about the other. There are some things we all know infallibly, about which we are certain. I know that I exist, that you exist, that I am here to-night speaking to you. Authority accompanies knowledge always. The man who *knows* any thing becomes necessarily a leader in his department, and all take him as an authority. There is no hesitation in his tone, no theorizing in his statements, no confusion in his speech, no cloud on his thought. And just so Jesus speaks of spiritual things. When he says, "Blessed are the poor in spirit, for theirs is the kingdom of heaven," he is stating a law of God's universe. When he says, "Not a sparrow falls to the ground without your Father," he states another law. Because the world recognizes in him this perfect insight, this clear vision, this infallible intuition of truth, it accepts him as its prophet, and sits at his feet as the great teacher of the race.

Fourthly. He came to bring sinners to God, to bring pardon for sin, to make those who were afar off nigh, and to fill the human heart with a serene and blessed peace. This is his atoning or priestly work. I care not for any of the theories about it, — I think them inadequate. I do not think, as the orthodox doctrine taught for the first thousand years, that Christ died to pay a ransom due to the devil; nor, as was taught for the next five hundred years. that he died to pay a debt due to God; nor that he was a sacrifice in the Jewish sense of a sacrifice. I believe more than all this; in an atonement larger, deeper, more universal, more in accordance with all Christ's teachings and the infinite love of God. I believe that Jesus, first of all men, clearly saw, and alone among men has fully declared, the infinite pardoning love of God to the sinner. He indeed teaches that God, when revealing himself in law, makes a perpetual distinction between right, and wrong, good and evil; that every man must reap as he sows; be rewarded and punished in this world, and in all worlds, according to his deed; be judged by his works; and, according to his practical fidelity, be ruler over five or ten cities; according to his practical infidelity, go into outer darkness. This eternal law of God, Jesus does not destroy, but fulfils, — carries out to its ultimates. But, meantime, he reveals the other side of divinity, showing the infinite tenderness and compassion of God, which makes no difference among his children, except this: that he cares most for those who need him most, so that there is more joy in heaven over one sinner that repenteth than over ninety and nine just persons who need no repentance. Christ's death did not produce this love, or make it possible for God to pardon sinners; but it revealed it. It showed that this love, binding the highest to the lowest, is the reconciling power in the universe, — the great atonement by which evil can be fully overcome by good.

While law divides and establishes a vast order of rank, power, position, love unites and penetrates all this majestic hierarchy with a divine attraction. Law unfolds the power of God, and displays his glory in creation. Love holds together in safety this infinite universe, and makes it all one.

This is the great atonement, which is taught everywhere in the doctrine of free grace, by which thousands and tens of thousands of sinners are brought to God. And this was, is, and will be the very centre of Christian revelation, — law made at one with love. And this great doctrine of the overcoming, all-conquering, omnipresent power of divine love to redeem the lowest and save the most abandoned, and lift the most forlorn, — this is nowhere taught as in the New Testament, and there only is fully reconciled with the equal omnipresence of divine law.

In my first chapter, I spoke of a soldier who, about to die, refused to say that he repented, or that he believed the atonement, because he thought if he did, it might be merely from fear of future punishment. Of course, I believe that sincere repentance is always necessary; and that whenever a man sees that he is going wrong, whether on the death-bed or at any other time, he ought to repent. He should turn from wrong to right: first inwardly, in his soul; then outwardly, in his conduct. But I commended the soldier for this: that he preferred to trust himself to God as he was, rather than to profess repentance and faith when he was not sure that he did repent or believe.

And, fifthly, I believe Jesus to have been Son of God, and Divine, — because filled full of the Divine truth and love, and always abiding therein. He alone, of the sons of men, was always resting on the Infinite love. He has sent the same spirit, in less degree, into the world, and enabled us all to say, "Our Father." His divinity did not consist in any technical or metaphysical deity of person, but in living in constant communion with God, so as to be a perpetual manifestation of the Divine truth and love. He is the unclouded mirror which reflects into the world the glory and beauty of the Almighty. Therefore, we all, beholding as in a glass the glory of God, are changed into the same image from glory to greater glory. Christ's divinity consists in being the image of the unseen God, — of God manifest in a man. God is manifest in Nature; he is also manifest in Providence, in history, in the intuitions of the soul. But in Jesus God speaks to us through human lips and a human life; and so, by our brother man, brings us to himself.

This, very briefly and imperfectly stated, is the truth I have been able to see in the supernatural view of Christ and Christianity, — dropping the non-essentials and retaining the essentials.

Turn now to the opposite doctrine, which stands at the other extreme of thought, which rejects the whole system of orthodoxy, and with it rejects also Christianity, and loses faith in the sublime personality of Jesus.

What shall we say of this?

It will not do to say, as is commonly said, that all such doubts and denials proceed from an evil heart of unbelief. I have seen and known numerous infidels in all parts of the land, and know that among them are many of the most upright and conscientious of men, whose lives would be a credit to any Christian church. What causes such men as these to become aliens to Christ? I think that their rejection of Christianity often comes from mistakes of the Church itself in making non-essentials into essentials, and constituting those doctrines a part of Christianity which do not really belong to it. For example, they object to supernaturalism, but to what kind? It is to Christianity, when considered as an interruption of the order of things, — an interference by the Almighty, to cure the evils which had come into the world. This sort of supernaturalism has been taught by theology, but where is it taught by Christ or his apostles? With them Christianity is no such temporary expedient, no afterthought, but was in the beginning with God, was before Abraham, was foreordained before the foundation of the world. The supernaturalism of the New Testament tells us of that Infinite Creator who, *above* nature, is for ever pouring his life *into* nature, "from whom, and through whom, and to whom are all things." Christ and Christianity were the supplement of all that went before, coming in the fulness of time, prepared for by all past history, announced by all past prophecy, and taking their place on the stage of being in accordance with universal law. And with this true supernaturalism true naturalism can have no quarrel.

Again, naturalism objects to the Miracles of the New Testament; but only to miracles when considered as violations of the laws of Nature, or considered as evidences of truth. But these definitions are the explanations of theology, not of the New Testament. The miracles of Christ are never called violations of law, but rather wonderful actions showing wonderful power. They are "single examples," as has been well said, "of laws boundless as the universe." And, so far from using miracles as proofs of his truth, Jesus rebukes those who asked for such evidence; saying, "A wicked generation seeks for a sign, and no sign shall be given it." He also appears to teach, in his parable of the rich man and Lazarus, that one who is not convinced by the truth without a miracle, cannot be convinced by a miracle. The rich man, pleading for his brothers, says: "If one went from the dead to speak to them, they would repent." To this Father Abraham is made to reply: "If they hear not Moses and the prophets, neither would they be persuaded though one went from the dead." That a being endowed with such exceptional power as Jesus should have performed wonderful works, naturalism cannot reasonably deny. But naturalism is right in maintaining that the God of Nature will not violate his own laws.

And, again, naturalism objects, and justly, to any conception of the divinity of Christ which makes it physical instead of moral. Christ is not divine by manifesting the omnipotence and omnipresence of God in the physical universe, for this was not his mission. He was divine in revealing the spiritual laws of God, and becoming a mediator of the divine love and truth. The Moral Law came by Moses; physical laws come by science; but grace and truth have come by Jesus Christ.

A shallow naturalism and a narrow theology may be at war; but a true science and a broad Christianity lend to each other a helping hand. When the world was believed to be in the centre of the universe, and all the stars to revolve around it every day, man, with his weakness, his ignorance, his feeble aspiration and faith, was also made the central object in creation. But how much nobler an idea we now have of the First Cause, who rules the immensities and eternities revealed by modern science! How theology is purified and elevated by every new access of truth! All this progress of the human mind only makes Christ seem greater, and Christianity more noble. A higher Christian doctrine is to come, for the Spirit is to lead the world on from truth to truth. A broader, more inclusive Christian faith is to elevate mankind. We are only now at the threshold of the great Christian temple which is to be. Christ is to be lifted up, and so to draw all men unto him. If Christianity shall ever die, it will only die as Jesus himself died, when it has finished the work given it to do. Only " when all things are subject unto him, shall the Son himself be made subject to him who did put all things under him, that God may be all in all."

What God has joined together let no man put asunder. God has joined together reason and religion, responsibility and freedom, faith and works, scientific progress and spiritual growth, the love of God and the love of man. Jesus, who is both Son of God and Son of man, is the natural leader of the human race. On the loftiest summit which the reason can climb, we still find him. In the lowest depths of human sorrow and sin, this great friend is still by our side. When our eyes close to all earthly sights, this divine brother is near us, to sustain and cheer with a hope full of immortality. As the world advances on the vast highway of progress, Christ will not become less human or less divine, but more so.

Sometimes, in reading the New Testament, I find the proof of the inspiration of the writer not only in the grandeur, but also in the subtlety of his thought. One instance of this is in the advice of the Apostle Paul to those scrupulous and somewhat narrow Christians in Corinth, who would not buy a piece of meat in the market until they had made sure that it had not come from the altar of Aphrodite or Zeus, where it had been laid as an offering. These punctilious Christians would not touch the meat which had been once put upon the altar of an idol. The liberal Christians in Corinth ridiculed them for this, and laughed at all such narrowness. Paul said: " Let not him that eateth despise him that eateth not; and let not him that eateth not judge him that eateth." The keenness of his intuition made the apostle select the precise words which in all times express the feelings with which orthodox Christians and liberal Christians are apt to regard each other. Narrowness *judges* breadth; breadth *despises* narrowness. The man who considers himself an advanced thinker looks with contempt on what seems to him stupid conservatism. The servant of the letter, on the other hand, denounces as an infidel and a heretic whoever walks in the freedom of the spirit.

Let us not judge each other, and let us not despise each other, but open our hearts to all the light and love which God shall send to us, knowing that we shall all stand before the judgment-seat of the eternal truth of God. When there, we shall have little cause to be proud, whether of our orthodox opinions or of our rational Christianity, but shall be grateful if God has helped us to be any thing or to do any thing for him.

III.

THE BIBLE.

WHAT is the Bible, and Where did it come from? "The Bible" means "The Book," and it is "The Book of books." No other scriptures of man compare with it for wide, deep, and ever-growing influence. It is the highest work of its class, — that is, of the sacred writings of mankind, and these sacred writings are, among all other writings, the most important and influential.

Every commanding race, every vast civilization, has been directed and controlled by its sacred writings. The hundred and fifty millions of Hindoos have been ruled, during twenty-five centuries, by their Vedas and Puranas. Chinese civilization has taken its stamp from "The Kings" and the "Four Books." The brilliant career of the Persian empire was inspired throughout by the Zend-Avesta. The tribes of Arabia were gathered, moulded, banded, and wielded in a resistless tide of conquest, by the Koran. The sacred books of the Buddhists have been the leaven of civilization among a third part of the human race during a vast period of time. If we judge them by their influence, these are the great books of the human race. But, for various reasons, the Bible stands above them all. The others are the books of particular races,—of the Hindoos only, or the Mongols, or the Persians, or the Chinese; but the Bible has a constituency composed of all the races of the world. The others belong to decaying, arrested, or dead civilizations; the Bible, to the advancing and all-conquering races, who stand for the highest civilization attained on this planet. The others are either narrow or shallow in some directions: the Bible is a fountain whose waters feed intellect, heart, life; promoting the highest worship as well as the largest humanity. This supreme value of the Bible has been recognized by thinkers of all schools. Walter Scott expresses the orthodox idea in the lines which he puts in the mouth of the White Lady of Avenel:—

> "Within this awful volume lies
> The mystery of mysteries.
> Happiest they of human race
> To whom our God hath granted grace

THE BIBLE. 59

> To read, to hear, to hope, to pray,
> To lift the latch and force the way;
> But better had he ne'er been born
> Who reads to doubt or reads to scorn."

Another writer, who is not usually supposed to reverence the Bible too much, — Theodore Parker, — thus speaks of it. I gladly quote his words to show that he is not that merely destructive radical he is often believed to be: "This collection of books has taken such a hold on the world as no other. The literature of Greece, which goes up like incense from that land of temples and heroic deeds, has not half the influence of this book from a nation alike despised in ancient and modern times. It is read of a Sabbath in all the ten thousand pulpits of our land. In all the temples of Christendom, its voice is lifted up, week by week. The sun never sets on its gleaming page. It goes equally to the cottage of the plain man and the palace of the king. It is woven into the literature of the scholar, and colors the talk of the street. . . . It blesses us when we are born, gives names to half Christendom, rejoices with us, has sympathy with our sorrowing, tempers our grief to finer issues. . . . Now for such effects there must be an adequate cause. That nothing comes of nothing is true all the world over. It is no light thing to hold, with an electric chain, a thousand hearts, though but an hour. What is it, then, to hold the Christian world, and that for centuries? . . . Some thousand famous writers come up in this century, to be forgotten in the next. But the silver cord of the Bible is not loosed, nor its golden bowl broken, as tens of centuries go by. . . . There must be in the Bible mind, heart, soul, wisdom, and religion. Were it otherwise, how could millions find it their lawgiver, friend, and prophet? Some of the greatest of human institutions seem built on the Bible: such things will not stand on heaps of chaff, but on mountains of rock." (Discourse of Religion, pp. 302–304.)

If, then, we ask, "What is the Bible?" the answer is, "The Word of God." But this answer takes two shapes, which I am now to consider.

One answer — and that the most common in the Protestant church — says: It is "the Word," by being inspired throughout by God, in every book, every page, every chapter, every verse, every word. It is infallible all through. Every part is consistent with every other part, and with all truth. If it contradicts astronomy or geology, so much the worse for them. If it contradicts historic monuments and records, then they are false. If it seems to contradict itself, this is only in appearance. It is the Word of God throughout,— from Genesis to Revelation; and "better had he ne'er been born, who reads to doubt" a word of any part of it, from Genesis to Revelation. This is the theory of infallible verbal inspiration.

The other answer to the question, "How is the Bible the Word of God?" is that it is filled with the Spirit of God. As we read the Old Testament, we everywhere feel the presence of divine power and justice ruling the world. The world and its affairs are all guided and governed by God, who will reward good and punish evil. It is a revelation everywhere of Divine law. As we read the New Testament, we are in the presence of a heavenly Father of an infinite tenderness, who pours blessings on the good and the evil, and desires to save every child. The Old Testament is inspired by the sense of Divine law, the New Testament by the sense of Divine love.

But its unity, its sacredness, its power, is of the spirit, not the letter. There is no infallibility about its geology, astronomy, or history; but its spirit is everywhere one. This spirit is developed more and more from the earliest to the latest books. The Old Testament grows more spiritual in the Psalms and Prophets than in Kings and Chronicles. The New Testament comes to fulfil the Old, — not to contradict it, but to complete it. The summit is reached in the life and words of Jesus, which are full of the highest truth.

In order to discover which of these views is the true one, we must see where the Bible came from. Our Bible is the English Bible. But the English Bible is a translation, for the Bible was written originally in Hebrew and Greek. Therefore, if the doctrine of verbal inspiration is true. not only must the authors have been miraculously preserved from error, but the translators also. Our present English Bible is a translation (called the Authorized Version), made by fifty-four scholars by the command of James the First. They were not left free to translate according to their conscience and knowledge, but were ordered to follow certain rules. They were not allowed to make a new translation, but only to correct an older one. They took the liberty of translating the same Hebrew or Greek word sometimes by one English word, and sometimes by another. And now we ask whether they were infallibly inspired always to choose the right word in their translation? No one pretends that they were; but, if not, the whole theory of infallible verbal inspiration falls to the ground.

Take, for example, the Greek words, "krima" and "krisis," which are translated in our Bible sometimes "judgment," sometimes "condemnation," and sometimes "damnation." Our English Bible makes Paul say that he who eats the Lord's Supper unworthily "eats and drinks *damnation* to himself." But it does not make Jesus say, "For damnation I have come into the world;" but, "For judgment I have come into the world;" and yet the word is the same. Our translation does not translate. "This is the damnation, that light has come into the world;" but, "This is the condemnation." Here, too, the word is the same. So the word "hades" is translated in one place "the grave," and in other places "hell." If, therefore, we are to consider our English Bible verbally inspired, then the translators must have been inspired to decide whether in such texts it is hell that is spoken of, or only the grave. But, as no one believes this, it is certain that our English Bible, at any rate, cannot be verbally inspired.

How is it, then, with the Greek or Hebrew Bible, from which they translate it? As the books of the New Testament were written in the first and second century, and as printing was not discovered till the middle of the fifteenth century, it is evident that these books were copied in writing by scribes during thirteen or fourteen hundred years. Were these copyists all infallibly inspired. so as to make no mistakes? Certainly not; for then the manuscripts now extant would not differ from each other as they do. In the 1,500 manuscripts of the whole or parts of the New Testament which have been compared together, more than a hundred thousand various readings have been found, — mostly unimportant, but some of great consequence. Now, unless some one is infallibly inspired to distinguish between these various readings, we cannot have a verbally inspired Bible. If you open your New Testament at 1 John v. 7, you will find the following verse: "There are three that bear record in heaven, the Father, the Word, and the Holy Ghost, and these three are one." This passage is the only one in the New Testament in which the doctrine of the Trinity seems to be plainly taught. And this passage is wanting in *all* the Greek manuscripts except two modern ones; in all the ancient versions; even in the copies of the Vulgate, before the tenth century; in all the Church Fathers, — even those who were discussing the Trinity, and who quoted the verses before it and after it; and is now universally admitted to be no part of the Epistle of John. Yet it stands in all our English Bibles, and is read and quoted as if it were a part of the inspired Word.

But let us suppose that somehow we have certainly possessed ourselves of the original text of the inspired writers: there is still another question. Who collected the books of the Old and New Testament, and decided that these were the inspired writers? In other words, who fixed the canon? Who was infallibly authorized to say that these particular books, and no others, out of all Jewish and Christian literature, should be put together in the Bible? The answer is, No one. The Bible was not thus formed. It came together gradually, on the principle of the survival of the fittest. Books which were at first a part of the Bible dropped out of it. Others, which were rejected by many at first, have finally become established in the canon as a part of the sacred Scriptures.

Not long ago, in the convent of St. Catherine

on Mount Sinai, a Russian scholar discovered an ancient MS. of the New Testament, which proved to be the oldest known. It goes back to the fourth century, and one way by which its age is determined is that it contains, among the other books, the Epistle of Barnabas, which ceased to be a part of the New Testament after the fourth century. Barnabas was the companion of Paul, and is called a prophet in the New Testament, and is said to be a good man, full of the Holy Ghost and of faith. He was sent to Jerusalem with Paul to attend the first Christian council. He joined the church at the very first, and showed his zeal by selling his land and giving the proceeds to his needy fellow Christians. He introduced Paul to the church, went with him on his missionary journeys, and is called an apostle in the New Testament. Now, an epistle, believed to have been written by him, was, for this reason, put among the Scriptures of the New Covenant, and remained in them two or three hundred years. Then it dropped out, — and, if you wish to know why, read it and you will see. Not because of any doubts entertained in those days of its authenticity, for it was repeatedly quoted by Clement and Origen as a genuine work of Barnabas. But it is full of tasteless allegories, — it has no weight, no substance, — and evidently it was left out of the New Testament because it was not fit to stay in. What books belong to the New Testament has not been settled even now. The Roman Catholic church puts into the Bible the Old Testament Apocrypha, which most Protestants reject. Criticism has not definitely settled in regard to two or three of the books of the New Testament, whether they are genuine. How, then, can we pretend that every part of the present Bible is infallibly the Word of God?

Another objection to this doctrine of verbal inspiration is that it repels many persons from Christianity, and is the cause of much infidelity. There are often honest and intelligent men who cannot receive the geology or astronomy of the Book of Genesis, or many of the miracles of the Bible. They are told that if they do not believe that Joshua stopped the sun in his course, and that the whale swallowed Jonah, they have no right to believe in Jesus Christ. So they are rejected from Christianity. One remarkable illustration of this is to be found in the French philosopher Rousseau, whose name has been identified with infidelity, when he was, in truth, the most religious man among the great thinkers of his own time and land. In his book on education, "Émile," he gives his creed in regard to Christ. He puts Christ far above all other teachers the world has seen, and is ready to accept him as his master in religion, because of his wonderful life and death. "Do not compare him with Socrates," he cries. "Socrates died like a philosopher: Jesus died like a God." As to his miracles, says Rousseau, I can neither receive them as facts, nor can I reject them. I admit my ignorance concerning them, — they may have been true, — only I cannot say that I believe them. But I can believe in Christ on other grounds, — because of his wonderful character and marvellous teaching. On these grounds I can be a Christian. But this was not considered sufficient by the church, and he was banished from France because of this book and these statements. He went to Switzerland, and there, in a small town, in Neufchâtel, found a little Protestant church, which received him on his own grounds, and there he had a religious home, and partook with them of the Lord's Supper.

At the beginning of my ministry, I had a church in Kentucky. There I found many persons who were reputed to be infidels, and thought themselves so, and whose influence was against Christianity, simply because they could not accept the verbal inspiration of the whole Bible. One man I knew, one of the best of men, upright and honorable, benevolent and kind, who was called an infidel. When I asked him about it, he said, " Yes, I have thought myself so, and for this reason, — when I was young, I heard a minister say, taking a Bible in his hand, 'Every thing between these lids is the Word of God, and if you do not believe it you will be damned.' I said, · If this is Christianity, I must be an infidel.' But now I have changed my mind. I do not think that Christianity requires me to believe every word in the Bible, and so I can gladly be a Christian."

Why, then, is this doctrine of the infallible verbal inspiration of the Bible still maintained? Not because the Scripture itself claims any such infallibility : it does not. It is indeed said that " all Scripture is given by inspiration," but not that this inspiration is infallible. Inspiration is one thing, infallibility another. The great poets, Homer, Dante, Shakespeare, are called inspired, and truly, because they have an inward illumination which shows them forms of truth and beauty and goodness unseen by common men. But this inspiration does not preserve them from mistakes. It does not make them infallible. Take the four Gospels and compare them with each other. One spirit, one life, pervades them all: it is the life of Christ. But they frequently contradict each other in details. If you demand verbal and minute accuracy, their whole story falls to the ground, and we lose our Master. They differ from each other openly and frankly all the way through as regards outward incidents. But, as to the substance of the story, they are one. They differ as to the details of Christ's resurrection, but that he really rose from the dead they are fully agreed. If it is necessary, in order to believe Christianity, to have verbal accuracy in the Scriptures, one cannot believe Christianity at all. for the Scriptures cannot be verbally accurate when they differ even in unimportant minutiæ. But it is not necessary. What we need is to be certain as to the main facts of Christ's life, teaching, and character. And we can be certain of these, just as we are certain of the main facts in the life and character of Alexander the Great, Dr. Franklin, Julius Cæsar. General Washington. No one pretends that these writers from whom we derive our information concerning such persons were infallibly inspired, yet we are at least as sure of the main facts of their lives and character as we are of the main facts of the life of Abraham, Samuel, or David. We are *more* sure that Julius Cæsar crossed the Rubicon on his way to Rome, and that Dr. Franklin was in London before the Revolution, than that Jesus went to Jerusalem at the beginning of his ministry; for all writers are agreed as to the one, and the four Evangelists are not agreed as to the other.

Many arguments have been brought to prove the theory of verbal inspiration, some of them very ingenious. But the difficulty with them all is that they merely aim at showing that the Bible *ought* to be verbally inspired, not that it is so. The fact remains that it is *not* so inspired, since it is in some places opposed to science, in others to history, and in others to itself. One curious fact shows that this doctrine is supported by the fear that, if a single verse of the Bible is admitted to be unsound, the authority of the whole will be gone. Scholars of all denominations admit that there are mistranslations and interpolations in our Bible which ought not to be there. Some years ago, the Committee on Versions of the American Bible Society, containing eminent scholars, all of orthodox denominations, prepared an amended edition of the English version. They did not make a new translation, nor amend the errors of the old one, nor even improve the text where it is admitted to be faulty. They only corrected some palpable misprints, and altered the headings of the chapters where these are incomplete or false, or where they are, in reality, comments on the Scripture. This amended version, indorsed by the secretaries, and adopted by the Board of Managers, was printed and circulated by them during seven years, and was then suppressed. This was done in consequence of a clamor, raised not merely by the ignorant, but in which even Reviews, Ecclesiastical Bodies, and Auxiliary Societies, did not hesitate to join. I asked one of the gentlemen, who was a member of the committee, why this was done ; and he said that it was owing to the fear that, if we once began to make corrections in the Bible, the people might lose their faith in it, altogether.

It is said, " Unless we believe the Scriptures infallibly true, there can be no *authority ;* and we need some *authority* to rest upon, otherwise all will become uncertain : and then there will be no firm convictions about any thing." I admit that we want firm religious convictions. I go further: I say we need to *know* spiritual things just as we know natural things. But I contend that the belief in a verbal inspiration does not give us that knowledge, but rather hinders it. I also maintain that we need to trust in the authority of Jesus. It is an immense help to have confidence in him as the way, the truth, and the life. But to trust in the *authority* of a teacher is not knowledge: it is only the door to knowledge. You send your child to school, and it is right that he should trust in the teacher's authority and take what is taught on that authority. But, if it ends there, he has not learned any thing. Until he has made his teacher's instruction a harmonious part of his *own* knowledge, he does not know.

Authority is a door by which we enter the vast temple of truth. It is a guide who leads us through the wilderness to the Promised Land. But there its work ends. It does not give us knowledge, — only the access to knowledge. The true authority of the Scripture is this, that it is a book made sacred by the love and respect of many generations. — a book which has brought comfort and joy to thousands and tens of thousands of hearts, — which has been the means of converting sinners and of edifying saints. Hence we ought to approach it with trust, expectation, confidence, and read it to find what it has to teach us. — seeking for the spirit of life and truth which is in it. But, to have this faith in the Bible as full of truth, it is not necessary to believe in its perfect accuracy in every respect, nor that it has been preserved by a miracle from all error. No one believes that Humboldt was infallibly inspired; but what authority his words carry! No one believes that La Place was infallibly inspired to write the " Mécanique Céleste." It has been said that in America not five men can understand it; yet his views of the universe are accepted by all. No one believes the " Nautical Almanac" an inspired book; but it is such an authority that thousands of vessels trust themselves to its calculations, and thousands of lives and millions of property are confided to its accuracy.

The true inspiration of the Bible is not of the letter, but of the spirit. Until we have caught that spirit, all the dogmas of its inspiration avail nothing. When we have that, we do not need them. The spirit of the Bible is one all through. From Genesis to Revelation, there is a sense of the power of God. It all brings us near to him.

Every thing is looked at as if he were near by. The book of Genesis teaches that God is the creator of all things. The Persians said that the stars and planets were gods. Genesis says: "God made them all." The Egyptians said that plants and animals were gods. Genesis says: "God said, Let the earth bring forth herbs and animals." It does not teach geology, but monotheism.

Pass on to the stories of Abraham, Isaac, Jacob, Joseph. What inspiration is there in these? you ask. Of the letter, none; but there is the spirit of trust in a providence, near by, guiding human feet evermore. Come down to David. He was a fierce soldier, a wild, passionate man, with many faults; but amid them all there was a love of right and goodness; there was a profound sorrow for his sins, and a perfect trust in God. When David, tending his sheep on the hillsides of Judæa, sang his song of trust, and said, "The Lord is my shepherd," the Divine inspiration taught him a strain which will echo through all time.

Then turn to the prophets. They were stern and solemn figures, — awful and venerable shapes, — "going in the heat and bitterness of their spirit." But they were firmly convinced of the ever-present Divine power. They stood like a rock, hoping against hope. They cry out to a backsliding people, "Seek ye the Lord while he may be found." "It is he who hath measured the waters with a span, and comprehended the dust of the earth in a measure." This is the inspiration of the Old Testament. It is Divine power around us all, and Divine law above us all, and Divine providence guiding us all.

In the New Testament, there comes another sense of sunny piety, — a happy atmosphere of heavenly love. Listen to Jesus: "Not a sparrow falls to the ground without your Father; and ye are of more value than many sparrows."

"Be ye children of your Father in heaven, who causes his sun to rise on the evil and the good; and sends his rain on the just and the unjust."

"Consider the lilies how they grow." "If God so clothe the grass of the field, how much more will he clothe you."

"I am the resurrection and the life. He that believes in me" — that is, who accepts my truth and trusts in my word — "shall never die." He does not die: death is nothing to him. He passes on and up.

"Neither do I condemn thee; go and sin no more."

"What man among you being a father, if his son ask bread, will give him a stone? How much more shall your heavenly Father give his holy spirit to those that ask him."

Is a theory of plenary inspiration necessary to enable us to believe the Sermon on the Mount or to utter the Lord's Prayer? Are not such sayings their own authority? And what did Paul mean when he said, "God has made us able ministers of the New Testament, *not of the letter, but of the spirit*, for the letter killeth, but the spirit giveth life"? What did he mean but exactly what I have been contending for here? Do I need any theory of verbal inspiration to be satisfied that he was filled by a Divine spirit when he said: "I am persuaded that neither death nor life, nor things present, nor things to come, can separate me from the love of God in Jesus Christ"?

Peter and James and John are not repetitions of Paul: they all speak in their own language, but one spirit runs through them all. When John says, "He that loveth dwelleth in God;" when James says, "Pure religion is to visit the fatherless, and to keep one's self unspotted from the world," — they said the same thing which Paul said in declaring that "Love is the fulfilling of the Law," and that Love is greater even than Faith or Hope. And all agree with the great words of Christ, when he taught that the chief commandment is to love God and love man.

The spirit of the Bible is one: there is no contradiction, no opposition there. But when Paul says, "The letter killeth," he utters a solemn warning; for care for the letter has always brought a chill of death to the soul.

It is not, then, because we wish to have less respect felt for the Bible that we oppose this theory of the letter, but because we wish more. If this whole theory were dropped, we should, as I am convinced, enter far more into the spirit of the Bible. The Bible would then no more be regarded merely as a master, but rather as a friend. Multitudes, now repelled, would be attracted toward it, and the Bible might say to Christian believers, as Jesus said: "I call you not servants," blindly obedient to an unintelligible command; "but I call you friends," intelligently obeying what you see to be right, intelligently accepting what you see to be true, and able to comprehend what is the length and breadth and depth and height of the love of God.

The power of the Bible is not in its letter, but its spirit. That spirit needs no support from dogmas or theories of a supposed infallibility. The Bible may be proved full of errors as regards science, — often wrong in its chronology and history. Its saints may be very imperfect characters; its prophets, mistaken in their predictions; its apostles, men of like passions with ourselves, and sometimes going astray. It may be true of them, as they said of themselves: "We have this treasure in earthen vessels, that the excellency of the power may be of God, and not of us." But what is the chaff to the wheat? The power of the Bible is that it brings God to man, and lifts man to God; that it shows a providence reaching through all history, and whose everlasting arms are below all things; a Father, whose love comes down into the heart of every child, who cares for us all, and is the Saviour of all. The Holy Spirit which pervades this book is *The Comforter.* It brings us comfort in our sorrows, light in our darkness, hope in our despair. When all the scaffoldings which surround the Bible are taken away, by which men have tried to prop it up, the world will begin truly to recognize its real glory. Kingdoms fall, institutions perish, civilizations change, human doctrines disappear; but the imperishable truths which pervade and sanctify the Bible shall bear it up above the flood of change and the deluge of years. It will for ever remain

> " A sacred ark, which from the deeps
> Garners the life for worlds to be,
> And with its precious burden sweeps
> Adown dark time's destroying sea."

IV.

THE CHURCH AND WORSHIP, — WHAT IS TO BECOME OF THE CHURCH? — ANSWERS OF THE SCEPTIC, THE SECTARIAN, AND THE BROAD CHURCHMAN.

THE subject of this chapter is, "The Christian Church, and what is to become of it?" And I shall consider three answers: the answer of the man who does not believe in the Christian church, — the sceptic; the answer of the sectarian; and the answer of the broad churchman. This question of what is to become of the Christian church, connects itself with the general subject of the essentials and non-essentials in Christianity; because only that which is essential in the church — if there is any thing essential in the church — will be found remaining in the future.

First, as to the sceptic. His answer is: "The days of the church have passed by. It is a dying institution. There will be *no* church in the future.

There will be no church," he continues, " because the foundations of the church have been completely undermined and overthrown. It has rested on the belief of its supernatural authority, as founded by God and Christ, and as essential to salvation. Its worship, its sacraments, its priests, have been believed necessary to save the soul. But this belief is passing by, and will soon be wholly gone. As the world grows more enlightened, its faith in this supernatural church and its authority passes away. In the coming years, there will be none so poor as to do it reverence.

"Besides," argue these reformers and critics, " what *need* is there of a church? We do not need its worship, — we can pray to God, and worship him alone in our closet, or in the groves which were God's 'first temples.' What need of listening to sermons, — we can read books, or hear lectures on science, literature, and art. What men want is knowledge, not ceremonies. Newspapers and magazines, lectures and colleges, are the teaching church of our time, to which all men go. Philanthropic societies and reform societies are the working church of this age."

"The church is not wanted," continue our critics, " and is even in the way. It usually opposes progress, opposes reforms. or else wholly neglects them. It leaves the abolitionist to free the slave ; the temperance societies to reform the drunkard : it turns over the blind and the idiots to Dr. Howe ; the ignorant children to Horace Mann ; the insane to Dorothea Dix ; the prisoners to the Prison Discipline Society ; our suffering brute relatives to the Society for the Prevention of Cruelty to Animals. Every one of these reforms lay directly in the way of the church, and it passed them by. The church should have preached deliverance to the captives. and emancipation to the slave ; the church should have preached knowledge for the people. should have carried help to the blind and deaf and insane and intemperate. It has notably failed in all these duties. Occupied with discussions about theology ; engaged in controversy about more or less water in baptism ; the exact consequences of Adam's sin ; the need of bishops to make a true church, or the proper sort of millinery to be worn by the priest, — it has omitted judgment, mercy, and faith. It cares more for anise and cummin than for love to God and man. In Europe. the Roman Catholic Church is to-day exerting all its power — as it always has done — to help the kings and the nobles and to keep down the people. In this country, there was one great overshadowing evil and wrong, — that of slavery, — and the church never did any thing to remove it, not even with the tip of its fingers. Away with such a church! we do not need it, and will have none of it."

I have stated this argument in its full force, for you can never satisfactorily meet an opponent, nor answer his objections, unless you first see and admit their entire weight; and I think we must concede that most Christian churches to-day greatly fail in this duty of curing the miseries, the wrongs, and the evils of the world. Occupied in making converts to a creed, or proselytes to a sect, or in awakening men to seek salvation from a future hell into a future heaven, they have neglected the hells around them here and the heavens that might be brought down upon earth to-day.

This is the account which Jesus gave of his mission, in his own town, in the presence of his friends and relatives, and at the beginning of his work: "The Spirit of the Lord is upon me, because he hath anointed me to preach the gospel to the poor; he hath sent me to preach deliverance to the captives. and recovery of sight to the blind; to set at liberty them that are bruised; to preach the acceptable year of the Lord." In our daily prayer, we are taught to pray that God's "will shall be done *on earth*." The work of Christ, as declared by himself, is to heal the woes and wrongs of this world; to bring liberty instead of slavery, peace instead of war. The highest, noblest name ever given to the church was when the Apostle called it " the body of Christ." When Christ was in the world, he had his own earthly body, — his feet, with which to walk to and fro, doing good; his friendly voice, speaking words of help and good will; his blessed hands, touching to heal; his eyes, full of love, looking on friends and foes with radiant benediction. Now he is no more here in outward form ; but his spirit is still here, and needs a body with which to act. The church is that body, — so says the Apostle : " Now ye are the body of Christ." Christ should look love, through the eyes of the church. on mankind; should heal with the hands of the church; the church should be his feet to go about doing good ; the church should be his voice speaking pardon and peace to the sinner. If it does not do this, it fails of its duty and neglects its work.

But what then ? Shall we say that because it has not done all its work it must be abolished and destroyed? Here I think our friends the critics are mistaken. Many, many years ago, when the abolition movement was comparatively young, I went to Hingham to attend an anti-slavery meeting. Coming back in the steamer, it grounded on the flats in the harbor, and we were obliged to stay on board all night, waiting for the rising of the next tide. Having no room to sleep, we held meetings during the night. Frederick Douglass was on board, and in one of his speeches he denounced the indifference of the church to the wrongs of the slave; and, calling it the bulwark of slavery, said that it must be broken down and destroyed before emancipation could come. I recollect replying that, admitting it was the bulwark of slavery, it need not follow that it must be destroyed in order that freedom should come. When, after the campaign of Leipsic, the allied armies arrived at Paris, they found it defended by Marshal Marmont with an army planted on the hill of Montmartre. This hill was then the bulwark of Paris. But the allied armies did not say, "We must destroy it; we must tear it down." No: they said, "Let us *take it*. Let us occupy it with our own troops." And thus, if the church were the bulwark of slavery, we did not need, and ought not to try, to destroy it, but rather take it and occupy it in behalf of freedom. That reasoning still holds good. The church is a power. The roots of it are planted deep in the heart of mankind. Grant that it is an imperfect institution. Let it then be improved. Others may call it, if they will, the Bride of Christ, the ark of safety, the pure and holy mother of souls, the infallible and spotless body. Let us rather name it, as Jesus did, a company of disciples, of children met to learn. The word *disciple* means simply a learner, a scholar. You do not blame a learner because he is ignorant. Ignorance is his qualification for learning. Christians may not be very wise nor very good; but, if they are sitting at Christ's feet to learn of him, then they are his disciples and members of his church. Men and women of culture and leisure, with opportunities for reading, for social intercourse, educated in principles of virtue, surrounded from childhood by examples holding them to goodness, breathing an atmosphere saturated with Christian influences, may not so much feel the need of the Christian church to keep them from going astray. But let them look round on society, and judge what would be the consequences if the institutions of religion should disappear.

By the census of 1870, it appeared that there were then in the United States 63,000 church edifices, with accommodations for 21,000,000 of people. In most of these churches, religious services are held every week. In 60,000 places in the United States, men and women and children assemble to recognize their relations to an infinite God, to be told of their obligations and duties, to listen to the words of the Bible. During one day in seven, the rushing tide of worldly cares is arrested, the hot struggle for wealth and power is calmed, and men look up out of time into eternity. In these 60,000 churches, people come together on the same broad platform of humanity, — the distinctions of life are set aside in the presence of God; parties, cliques, social separations have no place. Suppose all this to come to an end. The church fulfils the predictions of our critics, and disappears. No more Sunday rest, no more meeting for common prayer and praise, and for listening to the words of Jesus. Sunday soon grows to be like any other day, — and one monotonous, unbroken flood of work, care, study, amusement, sweeps through the year from January to December. Children are born, and no baptismal water consecrates them to God; our loved ones die, and no words full of immortal hope are spoken over them. The Bible, no longer read in public, is forgotten. It no longer stands as a Divine Law, commanding man to love his neighbor as himself; to overcome evil with good; to do justly, and love mercy, and walk humbly with God. Instead, we have the daily newspaper and the monthly magazine; instead of apostles, political editors; instead of prophets, lyceum orators. We shall have science, indeed, and art, and civilization; but will these supply the place of religion? Will chemistry and biology take the place of the love of God? Civilization is knowledge, wealth, luxury, art: but heap them up ever so high around you; abolish poverty, give comforts and luxuries to all, — have you abolished in the soul the need of God? The church alone, of all human institutions, speaks to us of immortality, of heaven, of an Infinite Father and Friend. It alone supplies the deepest need of the human heart, and is therefore built on a rock; and, no matter what storms of revolution or floods of change may come, it will not fall. The rock on which the church stands is not a creed nor a miracle; not a pope or a priest; not superstition, nor ceremony, nor habit: but the everlasting need felt by the earthly child for his heavenly Father.

European thinkers, alienated from the church, are excusable in not recognizing it as created by human needs; for there it is an establishment supported by the power of the State. But in this country no one is obliged to go to church, or to pay for public worship. Yet consider its progress here during twenty years. In 1850, there were 38,000 churches in the United States; in 1860, there were 54,000; and in 1870, 63,000. In 1850, the church property in the land was valued at 87.000,000 of dollars; in 1860, at 171,000,000; in 1870, at 354,000,000. During those ten years, which included the ravage and desolation of the civil war, the church property was doubled. This does not look as if the people of the United States think that the church is not needed, or as if it were soon to come to an end.

So much for the answer to the sceptic: now for the answer of the sectarian. The sectarian is a man who is persuaded that his own particular denomination is to swallow up all the rest. If he is a Roman Catholic, then *that* is to be the only church in the future. If he is a Presbyterian or a Methodist, then he believes all Christians are to become believers in the Assembly's Catechism or followers of John Wesley. If he is an Episcopalian, he calls that sect "*the* church," and somehow thinks that by calling it so he will make it so. If he is a Baptist, he cannot recognize any body of Christians as a church of Christ, wherein men are not baptized by immersion, and confession; and I ought to say — for we have sectarians among the Unitarians — that, if he is a Unitarian, he is likely to believe that the world are to be followers of Dr. Channing. Thus, while the census, which is truly catholic, tells us that there are 63,000 churches in the country, the sectarian Roman Catholic sees only his own 4,000; the sectarian Episcopalian, his own 3,000; the sectarian Presbyterian, his own 6,000; the sectarian Baptist, his own 13,000; the sectarian Methodist, his own 21,000.

These conceits are childish, and would be innocent, did they not weaken that union, co-operation, and brotherly love which are essential elements of Christianity. Sectarianism fosters spiritual pride; it lays stress on forms; it encourages making proselytes to a party instead of making converts to God. Instead of contending against evil, the churches fight with each other. Each tries to exalt itself at the expense of its neighbor, forgetting that those who exalt themselves shall be abased; forgetting, also, that if one member suffer, all must suffer with it. How foolish it is to suppose that any one denomination is to swallow up all the rest! If any one were likely to do so, it would be the Roman Catholic, — the largest, the oldest, the best organized of all. There is something imposing in its vast assumptions, in its unchangeable policy, its uniform aspect, in Europe or America, Asia or Australia. Many look with alarm on its rapid growth in this country, in numbers, in wealth and influence. Its organs speak with proud confidence of its coming power, when it is to conquer all the Protestant denominations and reign alone. An idle hope! If, in the sixteenth century, when it possessed all Europe, it was not able to resist the Reformation or to put it down, how can it succeed in regaining its power, when it is opposed not only by the Greek Church and the Protestant Church, but by the progress of civilization and the spirit of the age? As one church among many, it has done great services, and can do more. But, by claiming too much, it is in danger of losing all. The nations which rejected it — Germany, England, Scandinavia, Russia, and the United States — have advanced from weakness to power, and have become the leading States of the world. The countries which clung to it — Spain, Italy, and Austria — have gone down from power to weakness; and these nations are now throwing off its authority, and are likely to become its most radical opponents.

Regarding the Catholic Church as a church, I respect its influence and wish it all success. Looking at it as a sect, seeking to conquer all the others, I regard it as pursuing an unattainable chimera. The success of every church, sect, party, is limited by its power of meeting certain human needs. There are men and women who are made to be Catholics; others made to be Methodists; others to be Presbyterians, Swedenborgians, Quakers, Episcopalians. Unitarians. Each man is benefited and made happy by being in the place which suits him, — where his mind and heart are most at home, where his soul is fed with meat convenient for it. Some men can be made better by one form of faith and worship, some by another. Therefore, we need *all* churches and *all* denominations, in order to meet all wants. There is the same essential truth and the same essential love in all. All teach the same piety and the same morality. They teach from the same

Bible, they sing the same hymns, they offer the same prayers. There is not one sort of honesty for Baptists and another for Methodists. Episcopalians and Quakers have the same kind of charity for the poor and sympathy with the suffering. There may be diversities of gifts, but there is the same spirit; and there may be differences of administration, but the same Lord; and diversities of operations, but the same God. Among all these varieties, there is one Lord, one faith, one baptism, one God and Father of all, who is above all, and through all, and in them all. No one church will swallow up the rest, so long as the Lord makes men different from each other in tastes and qualities of mind. A Methodist, happy when he can be moved emotionally, and have a good warm time, is chilled by the atmosphere of a Unitarian or even an Episcopal church. One man finds his joy in reading Swedenborg, while another would starve on that diet. Many members, but one body. We ought to rejoice that *ours* is not the only church, since we cannot feed all. We ought to thank God that, since *we* cannot become all things to all men, other things besides ours are provided, that all may be satisfied. Some denominations are the Master's eye and ear, with which he can see and hear; another his feet, with which he can walk; another his hand, with which to touch and heal. If the whole body were the eye, where were the hearing? If the whole body were hand, where the walking? Let not, then, the head say to the feet: "I have no need of you." For God hath set in the church, first, Roman Catholics; next, the Greeks; then the Lutherans; after that, Episcopalians. Baptists. or Presbyterians, for the perfecting of the saints, for the work of the ministry, for the edifying of the body of Christ.

I go some Sunday into an old school Presbyterian church, and sit down. It is communion Sunday, and the minister proceeds to "fence the table," as it is called; in other words, to say who must *not* partake of the Master's feast. I, being a Unitarian, am shut out. He can keep me from the bread and wine, symbols of my Master's truth and love; but can he keep me from my Master himself? No: if I have faith in Christ, the fences fall before it. I sit at my Lord's feet. I am blessed by his love. I hear him say: "Son, be of good cheer; thy sins are forgiven thee!" We are all one in Christ Jesus. The barriers have fallen away, and I am in the midst of my brethren.

Perhaps, then. I open the hymn-book, and, as I turn the leaves, I find in it hymns by Watts and Wesley, Heber and Montgomery, and the Roman Catholic Faber: and here, in the midst of this goodly company of psalmists and saints, I find, "Watchman, tell us of the night," or "In the Cross of Christ I glory," by the Unitarian, Bowring; or "Sleep, sleep to-day, tormenting cares," by the Unitarian, Mrs. Barbauld; and directly my Presbyterian friends begin to sing, "Nearer, my God, to Thee," by the Unitarian, Sarah Flower Adams. Then I say, the hymn-book is the type of the truly Catholic Church which is to be; for here are collected singers of every sect and every name; and, as on the day of Pentecost, they all speak in our own tongue, in which we were born. The hymn-book shows that piety, or love to God, is always essentially one and the same thing, in all churches, all sects, all lands, all times.

Mrs. Barbauld, whom I just now mentioned, has a little apologue to show that charity also, or love to man, is the same thing, in all sects and churches. A mother is walking with her little boy, on Sunday, in the streets of a large city. The street is filled with people, who turn into the different churches, — some into the Established church, some into the different chapels. And the little boy wonders why, since they have the same Master, they should go in such different directions. But when the services are over, and the people are on their way home, a man falls in the street with a sudden attack of illness; and then a Presbyterian runs up and lifts him from the ground, a Methodist runs for a doctor, a Baptist gets water and bathes his forehead; and the mother, turning to her little boy, says: "You see, my child, that, though their modes of worship are different, their charity is the same."

The broad churchman is one who sees and knows that all Christian churches are essentially one; that piety and charity are the same in all; and while every sect and denomination is an individual member, doing its own work, and having a right to its own place and sphere, it ought not to be separated from the rest. It is only in the lower conditions of organic life that organs can be separated from each other, and the animal continue to thrive. In the higher orders and classes, each organ is necessary for the perfect life of the whole. The Christian church is in a low condition when its different parts are disunited, — a foot here, a hand there, and the head apart from both. In the future and higher church, every branch will be more active in its individual sphere, and yet more vitally united with the whole. Their functions will remain different: their life will be the same.

In order to act efficiently, the church of the future must be thoroughly organized. But, in order to meet the wants of all parts of society, it must include every thing valuable that is in all existing churches. It must take in Catholics and Protestants, and have place and work for all who love God and his truth sincerely. The Roman Catholic church has union, but not freedom; the Protestant churches have freedom, but not union; the church of the future must have both. Its unities will be those of the early church, — "One Lord, one faith, one baptism, one God and Father of all, who is above all, and through all, and in you all." Its one Lord will be Christ himself; its one faith, trust in him; its one baptism, the answer of a good conscience towards God; its God will be the God and Father of Christ, who is the universal friend. All who so believe in Jesus as to co-operate in doing good and getting good will be received as his disciples.

The church of the future will contain differences of ceremony and ritual, and will allow perfect liberty of opinion. It may include the solemn liturgy and the extemporaneous prayer, the majestic anthem, and the Quaker silence. For some minds are most influenced by the one, and some by the other; so the future church, like the Apostle Paul, will become all things to all men, that it may save all. If there are those to whom the light seems more religious when dimmed by passing through richly colored and storied windows, it will provide for them the vast cathedral with nave and choir and transepts and lofty spire. If any are benefited by having their clergy dressed in surplice and stole, in having holy water and incense, the benign church will furnish all this, but not make any of it essential. But, meantime, it will be a teaching church, a working church, a missionary church: giving its strength to save mankind here as well as hereafter. Everywhere it will overcome evil by good, war by peace, hatred by love, error by truth, ignorance by light, vice by purity, unbelief by faith.

The church of the future will convert the heathen to Christ, not by threats and terror, not by denunciation or pictures of Divine wrath; but by making actual Christianity like that of Christ himself. When Christendom is lifted up to a higher Christianity, it will draw all men unto it. When the Christian world grows more pure, upright, noble, generous, then the fulness of the Gentiles will come in. The great evils and wrongs which now oppress humanity will melt under the influence of this Christian love, as the icebergs from the pole dissolve in the warm currents from tropic seas.

The time will come at last — long foretold by prophet and sibyl, long retarded by unbelief and formalism — when wars shall cease, and the reign of just laws take the place of force in the great federation of mankind. As soon as the church is at peace with itself and becomes one, it will be able to make the world also one. Christ will at last become in reality the Prince of Peace, putting an end to war between nations, war between classes in society, war between criminals and the State. In trade, instead of competition we shall have co-operation, and all industry will receive its just recompense. Capital will be reconciled to labor; science to religion; reason to faith; liberty to order; the conservatism which loves the stable past to the spirit of progress which forgets what is behind and reaches out to that which is before. This will be the coming of Jesus in the clouds of heaven with the angels of God, and the spirits of the just made perfect. This will be the new Jerusalem, coming down from heaven. This will be the tabernacle of God with men, when he will dwell with them and be their God. Then shall the Lamb of God be the light of the world, and the nations shall walk in the light of it; and there shall be no more curse, and no more night, and no more tears, but all shall drink of the water of life freely.

This great hope, so often disappointed, but for ever renewed, must at last be realized. It was dimly seen by the ancient patriarch herdsman, the founder of faith in one Supreme Being who might be the friend of man, to whom it was revealed, under the lonely stars which hung over Ararat, that in his seed all the families of the earth should be blessed. Further on, David and the prophets caught a clearer sight of the heavenly vision, and amid the rudeness of that primeval age declared that the time should come when the sword should be beaten into a ploughshare, and the heavens rain down righteousness upon the earth. Other races and nations had a like vision of a kingdom of heaven to come upon the earth.

Virgil caught it from the mysterious Sibyl, and declared that a new order of ages was to begin, when all crime should end, and peace return to the world. The Christian church has, from age to age, prolonged the song of the angels, of a coming glory to God and good will to men. It has declared that Christ is to return and reign upon the earth in love and truth. Philosophies of a more material type have also chanted this same hymn of hope for humanity. and prophesied an earthly paradise to come from communism or the survival of the fittest. Such a hope, for ever renewed, in spite of perpetual disappointments, must indicate some conviction in the soul, so deep as to assure its own fulfilment. Modern poets look to America, and declare that the star of empire takes its way westward, and that Time's noblest drama is to find here its stage and its triumph.

> "The seas shall waste, the skies in smoke decay,
> Rocks fall to dust, and mountains melt away;
> But fixed his word, his saving power remains;
> Thy realm for ever lasts, thine own Messiah reigns!"

V.

HOW DOES A MAN BECOME AT ONE WITH GOD?—CATASTROPHE AND EVOLUTION IN RELIGION.

THE subject of this chapter is "The Essential and Non-Essential Elements in Christian Experience; or, How does a man become at one with God?" I have also added the title of "Catastrophe and Evolution in Religion," as indicating the two most common views as to the way in which every man in Christ becomes a new creature. This latter phrase is borrowed from geology, in which the two prominent theories of the formation of the earth are that of gradual and continuous development, of which Lyell was the chief supporter, and that which declares that the earth came to its present shape after numerous catastrophes, of which, among others, Clarence King has recently pronounced himself an advocate. As there are these two hypotheses as to the method by which the primitive, chaotic world became a new creation, so there are two similar theories concerning the process by which the chaos in the human soul is transformed into a cosmos of order, and man is changed into a new creature. The church usually teaches that man has fallen into sin, and that his nature has become so depraved that every human being begins his moral career with an inevitable bias to evil rather than to good. However much the old doctrine of natural and total depravity may have been softened, every denomination claiming to be orthodox declares that every child is fatally inclined toward evil rather than good. Therefore, in order to become a child of God, he must be radically changed. He must become convinced of sin, sensible of guilt, filled with penitence; and then, inspired by faith in the promises of the gospel, he must become converted, and so be made a new creature. Such an entire and radical change is usually violent, sudden, accompanied with deep convictions. When completed, the whole heart is changed, — the man now loves what he hated, and hates what he before loved. After this, his life is wholly altered; having done wrong and gone wrong before, he now begins to do right and to go right, and is in truth and reality a renewed and transformed person. It will be seen that the logic of such a radical change is derived from the assumption of a universal primitive tendency to evil rather than to good. Grant this, and it follows that a catastrophe must take place when man is converted, — a beneficial and blessed catastrophe indeed; like those which changed the raging fires, boiling oceans, and bare strata of the ancient world of death, into these fertile plains, forests and seas, full of life and joy.

Every deep and long-held belief at last passes into language. Thus in the popular churches it is assumed, in the language of the pulpit, that all mankind are divided into two classes, the penitent and impenitent. the saints and sinners, the converted and unconverted, the Christians and the unchristians. As the people come out of the world and approach the gates of the sanctuary on the Lord's day, they seem very much alike: with no great difference among them. There are good people, and people perhaps not quite so good as they; but it is impossible for any man outside the church to draw a line which shall divide them all into two classes. But the moment they enter the building, and the clergyman looks down upon them. at once they are divided into " my penitent hearers " and my " impenitent hearers;" and are spoken of as converted or unconverted, just as they would be spoken of as Germans or Irishmen or Americans. The chief object of the church in all its work is to change the second class into the first, to convert sinners, and to bring them to repentance. It is assumed not only that this vital and radical change is to take place in all persons before they can be regarded as God's children. but also that it is an evident and apparent one, that you can tell a converted man from an unconverted one, just as you can tell a Frenchman from an American. Moreover, this belief when established works its own fulfilment. If children are taught from the first in their Sunday schools and churches that they are children of wrath, that they are radically sinful by their very nature, that they do not love God and cannot, until they are essentially changed, — what is the natural result? That they do not try to do what is impossible, — they consider themselves outside of the kingdom of heaven. God is not yet their friend, nor Christ their Saviour, — not till they are converted. If they die unconverted, they die without hope. One of two things, then. They become careless and indifferent, hoping to be converted at some future time, but meantime meaning to enjoy this world as much as possible. Or else they try to be converted, and pray and agonize to pass through this mystical experience, till at last a reaction takes place, some rest comes to their mind, some comfort to their heart, and they joyfully take this as a proof that God loves them, and that they are converted to him. Then they, too, will always think that conversion is something sudden and painful, and will hold to the theory of catastrophe in religion. Generalizing their own history, they will assume that no religious experience is genuine which is not stamped with such marks as these.

And now we ask, What truth is there in this doctrine? It is certainly true that no man can serve two masters. Every one must be going in the right way or the wrong, aiming at truth and good, or not aiming at it. There is always some ruling motive in the soul, some chief purpose, eminent desire, overruling wish, to which, in case of conflict, all others must give way. Any psychology which ignores this fact is fatally deficient. Man was made, not to drift, but to steer. He must choose the good, and refuse the evil. If he does not do so, he virtually chooses the evil; just as a citizen who does not mean to obey the laws is at heart a criminal, ready to disobey them when any occasion comes. In an army, a soldier who does not mean to obey, means to disobey; and is at heart already mutinous. In a nation, a citizen who does not mean to obey the government is at heart a rebel. So a human being, in whom God has placed a conscience, making distinction between right and wrong, if he does not mean to obey his conscience, disobeys it. In this sense, it is certainly true that he who is not with God is against him. And in all such cases a change, to be thorough, must be a deliberate, conscious decision to do right and not wrong henceforth and always.

Again, it is very certain that a large number of people, even in Christian communities, have no determined purpose of right-doing. Their highest rule is not the law of God in their conscience, but some human law, public opinion, or personal convenience. They are not steering, but really drifting. They have no infinite Master whom they obey, no infinite Father whom they love, and therefore cannot be considered as having any Christian aim. They are children of the world, not children of God. As long as it is easy to do right, they will do it; as long as it is prosperous to be just, they will be honest. But when the rains of adversity descend, and the floods of temptation arise, and the winds of trial blow, they will be likely to fall, for they have no rock of a divine conviction and faith under their feet. Now, these people, though they may be very pleasant and agreeable persons, really need to be converted, just as much as any convict in the State prison, for they are no more serving God than he is. It will not do to assume that all respectable, decent, and well-behaved people are necessarily going the right way. They may be really going down, not up, — slowly, insensibly perhaps, but steadily. And, if so, then they must be called upon to repent, and to make themselves a new heart and a new spirit. And that will probably be a sudden change, even though it may not be a public or open one. It is, therefore, no wonder that there should still be so much of what I have called catastrophe in religious experience. To one whose mind has not been imbued with the sight of eternal realities from childhood, their coming must be often like that of the earthquake, the fire, the hurricane, and the volcano, rather than that of the still, small voice.

What are the essential facts in this Christian experience? They are two, — the two which Paul declared to be the sum and substance of his preaching both to Jews and Greeks; that is, the essence of Christianity, when disembarrassed of any thing merely Jewish or merely Pagan. He tells the elders of the church of Ephesus that he had kept back nothing profitable, but had taught them in public and private, repentance toward God and faith toward our Lord Jesus Christ.

Repentance and faith, — these are the two poles of Christian experience, around which it must ever revolve. Call them by other names, if you will, — " sin and pardon ; " " determination to obey God, and trust in his love ; " " doing our duty, and praying for help to do it right ; " " law and grace ; " " works and faith ; " or, more largely generalized, " the sense of responsibility and the sense of dependence," — these are the two essential elements of all vital religion. Man, born with a conscience which gives him the idea of an eternal law of duty, of an everlasting distinction between good and evil, light and darkness, right and wrong, knows well that he ought always to choose the good and refuse the evil. This is the doctrine, not of Christianity or Judaism only, but of natural religion everywhere ; and this law of obligation is unchanging and everlasting. This law of duty, which is *above* man, is also *in* man, rooted and fixed in the very texture of his soul, and we never can escape from it but by fulfilling it. Conscience sits supreme in every soul, an absolute autocrat, claiming our entire allegiance. We can turn from it, stultify it with sophistry, sear it with sin ; but it is there always. ready to reawaken, — and its awakening is terrible. Then there may be a shock like an earthquake, and the whole soul may tremble to its centre, listening to that awful voice as to the trumpet of the archangel. If the man hearkens to it and determines to obey it, and to live for what is right at all hazards, that is the first step of Christian experience. This is repentance or conversion. It is turning and beginning to go the right way.

But that is not enough : that is only half of what all men need for spiritual life and progress. To determine to do one's duty, no matter how hard, in spite of all temptation, — that is the beginning, the *Alpha* of all religion. But what shall help us to fulfil this purpose? We are weak ; evil habit is strong ; we are beset by temptation without and within, and we cry with Paul, "To *will* is present with me, but how to perform that which I will I find not." We resolve to do right, and presently we do wrong. We find a law in the flesh warring against the law of the mind. We need help of some sort, strength to *do* what we resolve to do, for a resolution alone is not enough. Then comes the second great fact of Christian experience, "Faith toward our Lord Jesus Christ." And what is the essential thing in this faith? Is it any belief about his rank and power in the universe, such as the Greek theologians quarrelled about for three centuries? Is it any metaphysical speculation as to the precise way in which the death of Jesus made it possible for God to forgive sin? Is it any profession of faith, or verbal declaration, — as though merely saying something about Jesus was to save the soul? No. The saving faith in Jesus Christ is to believe as he believed, trust in God as he trusted, hope as he hoped, and love as he loved. Just as we eat and drink food, and it becomes a part of our body, — it is to eat and drink Christ, so that his spirit shall enter into ours, and be the life of our soul. It is to trust in that infinite tenderness in which he trusted; to receive that boundless compassion which Jesus made known; to be pardoned, comforted, and made at peace with God by the truth and the love of which Jesus was the manifestation. If I were to say that "God was in Christ, reconciling the world unto himself," I should say exactly what I myself believe. But I use the words in no dogmatic and doctrinal sense, but as expressing the fact that what we see of God, as shown by Jesus, is that which brings the soul to him, and fills it with his peace. When we see Christ as he was and is, we look through the character of Christ and see that of God; see, reflected in this human child, something of the love of the Infinite Father. This sense of God's pardoning and saving love is the *Omega*, as the sense of duty is the *Alpha*, of all Christian experience.

But now we must ask again, Is it necessary that this experience should come in a moment, suddenly, and with a great commotion of the soul? May it not begin in the earliest childhood, be increased gradually by Christian education, and thus grow by a slow but continuous process of evolution and development into its full power and efficacy? A large part of the church declares that it may. In the first place, this is taught by all the sacramental churches, — who believe that the unconscious infant begins its spiritual life when the baptismal water touches its brow and the benediction is pronounced over it. Admitting the doctrine of hereditary depravity, they escape its consequences by the ordinance of infant baptism. The baptized child has become a child of God, just as if it had never inherited the curse of Adam. Now, all that it needs is Christian education and Christian sacraments, to keep it from going astray. And if the only way of escape from the cruel theology which declares every human being to be born in sin, if the only escape from this were to believe that this taint is wiped away at once by the rite of baptism, then I should pray God to enable me to believe it, and I should be glad to join the Roman Catholic and the high churchman in this sacramental rescue of the innocents. Let the evil introduced by one false theology be cured, if possible, by another. Two theological negatives might thus destroy the negation.

The rational Christian, however, takes another and a better way. He admits the fact, apparent to all, that we do inherit bodily tendencies which may be temptations to evil. Both right-doing and wrong-doing become at last habits, and these habits become instincts, and are transmitted from generation to generation. But it does not follow that there is any irresistible bias to evil, or any tendency which may not be overcome by education and example. Faith in Christ requires us to believe that good is stronger than evil, and can overcome it. Instead of taking for granted that children must go wrong, let us rather show them that we expect them to go right. Let us believe that God has planted in every soul aspirations for goodness, capacities for generosity, the love of truth, the sense of justice, — and let it be the business of the church to develop these germs of a true life, — so that no painful conversion shall ever be necessary.

I suppose it is a matter of fact that the majority of all church-members, even in those denominations which lay the most stress on sudden conversions, have become Christians by education and slow development. It has been repeatedly declared, in Sunday-school conventions, that statistics show the majority of church-members to be the children of Christian parents, brought up from childhood in the faith and practice of the gospel. The theory may require them to be suddenly converted to religion : the fact shows that they were gradually educated to religion. The proportion of church-members suddenly converted to those who were educated is much as it was at first in the company of the Apostles. Paul was converted in a moment ; but the rest of the Apostles were educated gradually by the influence and teaching of Jesus, by keeping company with him, hearing his words, and seeing his works. At the last, there came to them on the day of Pentecost the tongues of fire, enabling them to preach the word with efficacy. But that could hardly be called their Christian conversion. It was the promised power from on high, given them for the preaching of the Word. This history of the Apostles therefore shows that the chief method of the church in bringing souls to God should not be by catastrophe so much as by evolution. We should grow up in all things into Him who is our Head.

Other arguments of the evolutionists, as we shall call them, who are in favor of bringing men to God by a gradual education rather than by a sudden conversion, are these: "Is there not," they say, "something unnatural in the very notion of these violent conversions? We admit that, if men have been estranged from God and Christ, living worldly, selfish, and sensual lives, they may find their return to the right way accompanied with a shock. If people have become lost in a forest, they may have difficulty in getting back to the road. But cannot Christians walk directly forward on the highway to heaven, from childhood? Is there not such a way? Did not Christ declare himself to be the way? According to the theory of catastrophes, there is *no* way, no regular method. The Apostles were called the servants of the most high God, who show the way of salvation. Modern Protestant Orthodoxy is in a most unsatisfactory attitude. The business of the church is to bring the world to God. Then it ought to know exactly how to do it, — how to begin, how to go on, how to finish. Such is the case with all other work. If a man is to build a house, he does not bring together his materials, hire his masons and carpenters, and, when all are ready, sit down and wait for some sudden shock or emotion by which they shall be enabled to go on with their work. If we are merchants, lawyers, teachers, blacksmiths, we do not wait for a revival before we can fulfil our engagements. It is only in converting the world to God, — the most important work of all, — that this strange system is adopted. Here, there seems to be no regular method of growth in goodness; but we must use the means of grace, and then wait for the result. Religion is to be obtained by some supernatural method, — by a spasm, an agony, a struggle, — not by any regular, practical work. If a man wished to become a Christian in the days of the Apostles, he went to them and said, 'What shall I do to be saved?' and they answered at once, according to his case, either, 'Repent and be converted,' — if he was committing some sin, — or, 'Believe in the Lord Jesus Christ,' — if what he needed was faith, — or, 'Be baptized,' — if what was wanted was an open avowal. But now, if one asks, 'What shall I do to be saved?' no one can exactly say what is to be done. There is a prolonged struggle, an agony, prayers, tears, — finally there may or there may not come relief and comfort. If these come, it is assumed that the man is converted; otherwise, he must wait and try again. All this confusion," say the evolutionists, " is the result of this false method of reliance on catastrophes. The Roman Catholic Church does better, for that commits no such blunder. No doubt, it admits revivals into its system, and has its seasons of extraordinary attention to religion. But it does not depend on them to create religion in the soul, but only to increase its glow and power. In the Roman Catholic Church, every baptized person is taught to believe himself a Christian, so long as he does not continue in mortal sin, but preserves his Christian life by a regular use of the sacraments. Every Roman Catholic who obeys the rules of his church is taught that he is safe and in the right way. In most Protestant churches, if its children born and brought up in it are Christians, it is, so far as theology is concerned, only a fortunate accident."

Another bad result of this method, say the evolutionists, is that it discourages some and inflates others. He who has not been able, for some reason, to obtain these inward experiences, considers himself as no Christian, having no part in the hopes of the gospel. He who has been through such an experience, and has attained a hope, thinks himself safe. He is safe, he believes, because of his past experience, not because of his present fidelity. He was converted at such a time, so he trusts that he is right. To work out his salvation by deeds of charity and by growth in goodness would, he thinks, be to rely on mere morality. Therefore, the members do *not* grow in knowledge or in grace, as they otherwise would. Hence, the reproach often made, sometimes unjustly indeed but sometimes justly, that church-members are no better than others. They are not taught that any thing depends on being better. Most stress is laid on conversion, little on progress. Thus, they are exposed to great temptation, and may be led into spiritual pride, which so often goes before destruction. Is it not possible, it is asked, that some of the moral disasters which have befallen leading men in the church are owing to the false security which such men have felt in consequence of this theory that Christianity consists essentially in being converted, not in leading an upright life? Therefore, say the evolutionists, a wholly different method is necessary. We ought to take our little children at the beginning, and, instead of trying to torture them by an effort to obtain a change of heart, teach them that they already belong to God and Christ, and that they are in the kingdom of Heaven now. Teach them that so long as they try to correct their faults, obey their parents, and fulfil their duties, they are in the right way. Teach them to pray to God, not as aliens or outcasts, but as his children, and to grow up from faith to greater faith. Make them understand that, while they are thus living in obedience and faith, they are in the peace of God, and have a right to all the promises and hopes of the gospel. Teach them that the work of life is to get good and to do good. Convert sinners by the same doctrine: make them understand that God is not hidden nor afar off; that he is not in some distant heaven, nor beyond some far-off gulf of space, but very nigh to us all, in our conscience and our heart, ready to help, to bless, and to save at every hour.

These are the two theories in regard to the way of salvation, — which is the true one? One of these theories, it will be seen, lays the principal stress on the beginning of the Christian life, — that is, on conversion; the other, on the development of the Christian life, — that is, growth in goodness. Now, according to any theory of Christianity, *both* are necessary. Is Christianity a journey, a "Pilgrim's Progress" to heaven? Then it is necessary to begin the journey, to be sure that we really are intending to go, and that we have begun to go. It will not do not to assume that all men are on their way to heaven. They must adopt a purpose, commence a work, begin to go, put themselves in the right way; and, until this is done. nothing is done. So far. the believers in catastrophes are right. But. on the other hand. what is the use of beginning the journey. unless we go forward? What good in being converted to God. unless we learn to obey God? The object of Christianity is to change this world into the kingdom of heaven; but the kingdom of heaven is not meat nor drink, but righteousness. peace, and joy in the Holy Ghost. It is to do justly and love mercy and walk humbly with God. Unless we enter this kingdom of truth and love, what good in passing the portal? The only advantage in beginning to go on this journey is that we should keep on and arrive at the end.

Is Christianity a life? Then, in order to live, we must be born; but, unless we grow up, what good in being born? The Christian life is one of faith, hope, love, obedience, — the life of God in the soul of man. We are born into that life by a determination to obey God and do his will. We grow up by daily obedience, daily trust. daily prayer.

This life, as we have seen, consists of two parts: one, which depends on ourselves; the other, which comes from God. The part which depends on ourselves begins with repentance and conversion, and goes on by continued well-doing. It is work, all through. The part which depends on God is all of grace, — it is from grace to grace, — grace all through. It was by the grace of God that Christ came. God so loved the world that he sent his Son, our brother, to show the way of salvation. It is by grace that he comes to us, and that we are born amid the promises and hopes of the gospel. It is God's grace which forgives our sin when we repent. It is God's grace which leads us to repentance by inspiring faith in his love. It is the grace of God which invites us to pray, and it is his grace which answers our prayers, takes the burden from the heart, and fills it with his peace. All we have to do in order to be saved is to work and to trust. There are no obscure mysteries to be believed, no awful burdens to be borne, no sin which cannot be pardoned if we repent, nothing to do but what God will give us strength to accomplish. We are saved by faith, and also by works. If we had not faith, we should not have the courage to work; if we did not work, our faith would soon die, — for faith without work is dead.

Genuine Christian experience, therefore, may be sudden or gradual, or both. *Conversion*, or turning round, is always sudden. If one is doing wrong or going wrong, he cannot too suddenly begin to go right. But going forward is gradual, growth is gradual, progress is gradual. The coming of God's life in the soul is like the coming of spring. A little while ago, all was cold and hard and dead. Now, a soft breath of warm odor fills the air, the life stirs in a million buds, the grass begins to grow green over a thousand miles of meadow and prairie, a wave of verdure rolls slowly up from the south over the northern forests. Every majestic oak, every little bush, shakes out its tender leaves to welcome the coming sun; insects hum, birds carol, the fish flashes through the stream. So is the coming of God's love and truth in the human soul. As the earth, in spring, turns itself upward toward the sun, so we turn our hearts upward to God in submission and trust. As the sun pours down his answering radiance, magnetizing every germ into advancing life, so the spirit of God descends softly into all willing hearts, creating a new vitality within. There enters the soul a sense of pardon, comfort, and peace; and out of this there come the flowers of beauty and the fruits of goodness. "The wilderness and solitary place shall be glad for them; the desert shall rejoice and blossom as the rose." "The parched ground shall become a pool, and the thirsty land springs of water." "And a highway shall be there, and a way, and it shall be called the way of holiness: the wayfaring men, though fools, shall not err therein."

On this deep foundation of Christian experience all Christianity rests. It is the solid rock beneath the church, — like Peter's faith, which flesh and blood had not revealed to him, but the Father which is in heaven. All belief in Christ and Christianity, founded on hearsay, which flesh and blood have revealed, is unstable. Human teaching; the authority of others; the belief of parents and friends; the outward blessings and advantages of religion, — these are only like John the Baptist, sent to prepare the way of the Lord. Not till we come to God ourselves, by personal submission to the law of right, personal trust in his all-sufficient love, do we have any solid Christianity. After that, if we speak, we speak what we know and testify what we have seen. If men fall away from religion and become unbelievers, it is because they have never really had any true religious experience. For what we have once seen, once known, of God, Christ, duty, love, immortal hope, is a possession for ever. Heaven and earth may pass away; but this Divine word, once seen and known, shall never pass away.

On this solid personal experience, the whole future of Christianity must rest. This is still the rock on which Christ builds his church, and which will for ever resist all that can injure or destroy. Out of this deep, broad, living Christian experience, shall come that future church of Christ which shall combine variety with unity, works with faith; which shall be broad enough to adapt itself to all human diversity, deep enough to satisfy all human needs; so progressive as to walk abreast with all human development; so aspiring as to bring down God's kingdom to this world and make heaven upon earth. But the Christian experience, out of which all this grand future shall grow, will be nothing narrow, nothing formal, and not a mere confused emotion. It will be the vision of God's truth and God's love, — the light of things eternal. It may come suddenly or gradually, but it will be always essentially the same. It will always consist in the sight of the Divine holiness, justice, truth, order, and law, — producing obedience, — and the sight of God's pardoning love, saving grace, spiritual influence to redeem and bless, — producing faith, hope, love.

VI.

WHAT ARE THE ESSENTIAL REASONS FOR BELIEVING IN A FUTURE EXISTENCE, AND WHAT WILL THAT EXISTENCE BE?

I HAVE to speak, in this closing chapter, of the essentials and non-essentials in regard to a future life. What are the essential reasons for believing in a future existence? First comes the remarkable fact that it has been the faith of the human race. In all ages, lands, civilizations, races, religions, men have believed in a hereafter. All the great religions have taught it, — Zoroaster and Buddha, from the far East, and from out of a gray antiquity; Brahminism; the religion of ancient Egypt, Greece, Rome; these all declare with one consent that, if a man die, he <u>shall live</u> again. Poetry, legend, romance, superstition, agree in looking out of time across that sea of one shore which we call death, and painting pictures of the other land which, as they take for granted, lies unseen beyond. The most savage races of Africa, or the islands of the Pacific, are haunted by the terrors of ghosts and spectres whose existence is a part of their fixed belief. And, when we ascend to the other extreme of the scale of human development, and commune with the demi-gods of thought, — with men made little lower than the angels, — we find the childish superstitions of the ignorant lifted into a calm faith in immortality. Among the events of this earth, that which, with one exception, touches our hearts most deeply, is the long conversation held by Socrates, on the day of his execution, with his disciples. This great truth-seeker devotes the last hours of his life to considering the arguments for immortality and the objections to it, and, having replied to all the objections, looks forward with confidence to another existence. Calm, wise, tender, without fear, he advances toward death, sure that death will only touch his body, not his mind. When sunset was near, he said: "Let the poison be prepared, — for it is best not to linger." Crito asked: "How should you like to have us bury you?" Socrates replied, with a smile: "Any way you wish, — if you can only get hold of me. Have I not shown you, Crito, that I, who have been talking to you, am not the other Socrates who will soon be a dead body? Do not say, then, at my funeral, 'Let us

bury Socrates,'— for such words are not only
false, but they infect the soul with evil." And
when we pass up from Socrates to one still greater
than he, — to the highest of all human souls, —
we find him saying not only that he is immortal,
but that he is immortality. Immortal life and the
resurrection, or the rising up of the human being,
these he declares to be the very essence and centre of the true man himself. "I *am* the resurrection and the life; he that believeth in me"—
that is, he who believes in that truth which is the
essence of my being — "he shall never die." In
other words, the soul itself is essential life, and
death cannot touch it.

I do not mean to say that this universal belief
in a hereafter has no exceptions. There have
always been a small number of doubters who have
not been able to accept this doctrine. There
have been two difficulties, and very important
ones, which have staggered them. First, there is
the impenetrable veil which hangs between us and
the other world. It is so strange that those noble
souls, so full of interest in this life and in human
affairs, should pass away and never be heard of
again; that those hearts, bound to us by an affection stronger than adamant, should leave us and

never come to us any more! If they were alive, if they were anywhere, should we not somehow know of it? This vast human procession moves steadily on, and the instant it passes that low portal of death it disappears from our knowledge for ever. This fact is one of the great difficulties in regard to a future life. True, there has always been a vague belief in ghosts, in apparitions of the dead, and spiritual manifestations; but these have been so vague as to be rather an alarm than an encouragement. Another great difficulty as to our continued existence is the dissolution of the body. All that we know of human life is in connection with body. Life in this world is inevitably bound to body. But death dissolves body, — how then can life continue?

Considering these two facts, (1) that we know nothing of the continued existence of those who have left us, and (2) that we know of no life here except in connection with body, it is not at all wonderful that men should have hesitated in accepting a future existence. But what *is* wonderful, and very wonderful, is that, in face of these two facts, the immense majority of mankind should yet have believed in immortality. This faith is a most amazing phenomenon, and is to be accounted for. Am I told that the wish is father to the thought? that men *believe* in a future life because they *desire* a future life? I reply that this merely changes the form of the wonder. We then ask, Why do men *wish* to live hereafter, if there is no hereafter? If all they know and love is here, why this universal wish for a continued existence in some unknown world? As Shelley says:—

> This earth is the nurse of all we know,
> This earth is the mother of all we feel,
> And the coming of death is a dreadful blow
> To a brain unencompassed by nerves of steel,
> When all that we know, and feel, and see,
> Shall pass, like an unreal mystery!

If, in spite of all the reasons for doubt, in spite of our ignorance concerning the future world, — there is a universal instinct in man to believe in such a world, — this instinctive belief is itself a proof that we are to live again. Every other instinct has its appropriate object. There is an instinctive desire for food, and food is provided; an instinctive longing for knowledge, and knowledge is given; an instinctive joy in beauty, and beauty is shed over the world; an instinctive social tendency, and society is here; an instinct for construction and art, and the means of exercising this are given. If, therefore, there is planted in man an instinctive longing for immortality, — universal, constant, permanent, — we may be sure that God provides an existence to satisfy such a longing.

As to the difficulty arising from the fact that bodily organization is necessary to all life here, — we see that, in spite of this, men have usually believed in a soul which may exist independently of the body. The belief in ghosts, just referred to, is evidence of this. A ghost is assumed to be a being without a body, yet capable of thought, action, speech; capable of being seen, of moving to and fro, of continued personal identity. In short, it is a soul existent without the bodily organization. Now, there either *are* ghosts, or there are no ghosts. If ghosts exist, then evidently the soul may exist without the body. But if there are no ghosts, then mankind has always believed it possible for souls to exist without the body, though they have no proof of it. This, therefore, must be an instinctive belief, and, like all other instincts, has something in reality corresponding to it. If, though there have never been any ghosts, men have always believed in ghosts, it proves that there is something within us which feels itself capable of existing without the body. And such a consciousness can hardly be explained except by assuming the reality of such a soul, which, using the body but as the means of communicating with this world, is capable of existing in some other way hereafter.

The first reason for believing in immortality is that we are made to believe in it. There is no better evidence than that a belief accords with human nature. But, beside this, is the fact that our confidence in immortality increases as we have more and higher life. In a low condition of our existence, death is the "king of terrors." But as man becomes more alive in mind, heart, spirit, death loses its sting and the grave its victory. This is one way in which Christ has abolished death, — by making the human soul more full of life. This is one way, and his resurrection is another. It is a fact, explain it as you will, that the disciples of Jesus were emancipated from all fear of death. *They* explained this phenomenon by saying that they had not only seen their Master alive, after his crucifixion, but also arisen, ascended, gone into a higher world; from which, nevertheless, he came to encourage them. It is often said that the resurrection of Jesus is the great *miracle* of Christianity. But I believe its power consisted in its *not* being a miracle, but a revelation to the disciples of what was to come to them all. *All* were to rise, as Jesus rose. They saw that, instead of death being a descent into a dark under-world, it was an ascent into a world of higher life and larger light. The power of the resurrection for the disciples was that it bridged the gulf between this life and the next, and showed them Jesus gone up to glory, victory, and heaven. And the power of Christ's resurrection to us is that the faith in a continuance and ascent of being has been transmitted in the church as a permanent possession, taught us in our infancy, breathed in with the very air around us, and reinforcing the original instinct of immortality.

I am not one of those who refuse to the lower animals all hope of continued existence. I believe it very possible that the living principle in the animal may be capable of development into some higher modes of existence after the death of the body. The reason why immortality is usually denied to animals is that their lives seem to be complete here. They have, apparently, no unex-

BELIEF IN A FUTURE EXISTENCE. 135

hausted capacities. The lower races of men are like animals in this, that they also manifest few tendencies reaching beyond their present life. But, as man's soul is developed by knowledge and culture, this surprising phenomenon appears, that while his body grows old and decays his mind continues to advance. The bodily life is limited to seventy or eighty years, — then it must decay, and at last perish. But no such limitation applies to the soul. The mind of Michel Angelo at sixty-seven accomplished one of his greatest works, and at ninety his powers were in full activity. Milton finished and published "The Paradise Lost" only a few years before his death. The mists of age may indeed dim the radiance of the soul, as clouds collect around the setting sun; but occasional gleams of glory show that the power is there, though partially hidden. These inexhausted and seemingly inexhaustible capacities are a sign that we are intended for further being. Problems open before the mind which the mind is incapable of solving in this world. These prophesy some other state where they can be comprehended. The undying affection of the human heart for the loved and lost reaches beyond the grave, and assures us of some future reunion.

When the reason is unable to prove an immortality, the heart asserts it on the evidence of its own imperishable love.

The word "indenture" came from the old custom of cutting a parchment contract into two pieces; divided, not by a straight line, but by a jagged one, marked with *indentations*, each party to the contract retaining one piece. If we were to see such a parchment, with the lines thus abruptly cut asunder, we should infer from their incomplete sense that there was somewhere another piece, which would make the meaning entire and intelligible. The mind of man, in this world, is such an incomplete parchment. Intellectual questions are roused, which cannot be answered. Moral difficulties appear, which are left unsettled. He has longings and aspirations for a good and a beauty which this world cannot supply. He sees all around him inequalities and apparent injustice; the triumph of evil, the defeat of goodness; bad men in power, patriots in exile, —

> Truth for ever on the scaffold, wrong for ever on the throne;

the false priest surrounded with admiration, the true prophet despised and rejected of men. Of the child of genius, born under inhospitable auspices, how often it must be said that —

> "He came and baring his heaven-bright thought,
> He earned the base world's ban;
> And, having vainly lived and taught,
> Gave place to a meaner man."

If this life were the whole, all such inequalities and discords would be inexplicable. In all ages, therefore, the conscience of man, no less than his reason and his heart, has predicted a future state, where the wrong should be made right, the triumphant falsehood exposed, injured innocence be vindicated, and the righteous judgments of God made known. The conscience does not so much demand retribution on the wrong-doer as vindication of justice and right. It predicts a revelation of truth and the exposure of lies.

I have seen a little infant die, — one just come into the world. As yet it had developed no character; it had no conscious intelligence; it was nothing but a promise, — an expectation. But that promise, that faint prophecy of a coming future, had so taken hold of its mother's heart that the loss of her infant nearly drove her to despair. But that infant was God's child too; more the child of God than of its earthly parent, for God himself had sent this bud of hope into the world. And shall the heart of the earthly father and mother cling thus to their darling, and the heart of the heavenly Father let it go for ever into emptiness and annihilation? Shall we, who have so little power over its destiny, struggle and cry and pray, and use all means to save it, and he who holds it in the hollow of his hand let it slip into an abyss of destruction? No! this yearning of ours for our loved ones is only a faint, far-off shadow of that Infinite love which envelops them and us, now and for ever.

I know very well what materialism replies to all this. It tells me that life, thought, love, are mere results of organization: that, when the organization perishes, these of necessity go too. A drop of blood in the human brain will put an end to the aspiration of the saint; the lesion of a nerve destroy the courage of a hero. The poet's eye, rolling in a fine frenzy, turns from heaven to earth, from earth to heaven. He is on the point of creating a Hamlet or the Iliad: a little congestion of serous fluid arrests the conception, and it is gone for ever. True. The body, while we live in it, is the indispensable condition of our activity. But it does not follow that we are the result of the body. Rafaelle, while painting the Dresden Madonna, might have been stopped by some trifling defect in his brushes, or his oils, or his canvas. But that does not prove that Rafaelle himself was the result of his implements. The body is the organization which, in this world, the soul uses, — without it, it is helpless. But that does not prove that the soul is the result of its organization.

I have seen, in this city, great crowds collect to follow the body of some eminent person to the grave. So it was when John Andrew died, so when Charles Sumner died. The sense of a great loss fell upon the city. Business ceased; the hurry of life was, for one hour, suspended. The whole community stood around these remains, once inhabited by a patriotic soul. And shall we, creatures of a day, thus mourn the loss of our human brother, — and shall the Infinite Love dismiss him into the night and void of annihilation?

One of the last great discoveries of science is that of the conservation of force. So economical is nature that she never lets go one atom of matter, one molecule of organized being, or one unit of power. All is changed, nothing is lost in the creation. But here is a soul, the greatest force of all, the fine result of a long series of developments; a soul capable of thought, of love, of intellectual creation. It is the soul of Newton, able to read the laws of the universe; the soul of Fénélon, reaching a height of disinterested love which makes it like the seraph near God's throne; the soul of Homer, whose song fills the world with music during twenty-five centuries. And do you tell me that, while not a particle of carbon or hydrogen can escape the omnipotent conservatism of the Almighty, he will allow such powers as these to be resolved back into nothing? With the religious man, this argument is all-sufficient. When we come to see God as a father and friend, death is abolished. We know that we can trust him with our life, and the lives of those dear to us, always. Therefore, the early Christians, hiding from the rage of their persecutors in the dark caves beneath imperial Rome, laid their dead away, and wrote over them inscriptions full of hope, love, and joy: "My dear Caius sleeps here." "Rest in peace, my Theodora." This same trust has come down through all the intervening ages, and is ours to-day, Now, as always, faith overcomes death, and wins the victory from the grave.

The greatest impulse yet given to belief in immortality has come from the divine trust of Jesus in God as the Universal Father, — the Father of the evil as well as of the good, — whose sun shines and whose rain falls on the grateful and on the unthankful. This relation of the father to the child is a tie which death may not sever. It goes below all distinction of character, of capacity, of worth. The father and mother do not love their child because it is full of power and promise, full of affection and goodness, *but because it is their child.* The pity of their hearts accumulates the more around the weakest, the least attractive of their children; the poor thing born with an irritable temper, a weak purpose, or some inherited tendency to evil. And when the feeble infant, worn out with disease, at last lies in its little grave, the parents' love goes with it still. Long years after, that undying love holds the lost child in fadeless memory. If, then, these poor hearts of ours cannot forget our children, does the Infinite Heart of the universe cease to remember them? If we do not love them less because of their weaknesses and incapacity, how much more shall the Father of their spirits look down on them with inexhaustible love. Say not that his infinite tenderness can be exhausted by their sin, when ours, so much poorer, does not grow faint nor weary. If we must forgive our brother, not seven times, but seventy times seven, when shall an Infinite mercy grow unrelenting and implacable? Our reason and conscience are disturbed by incompleteness and discord in this little world: shall the Perfect Reason permit an everlasting discord, an eternal hell of sin and misery to continue, unconquered by his love, unredeemed by his gospel, for ever? Jesus himself has taught us this mode of reasoning, by analogy, from the poor love of earthly parents to the vaster tenderness of the heavenly Father. The only argument Jesus ever used against the Sadducees in defence of immortality is founded on this high conception of the fatherly character of God. If he calls himself the God of Abraham, Isaac, and Jacob, then they must live; for whatever belongs to him cannot die. If he is not willing that any should perish, then no one can perish. Evil must be overcome at last by good; death must be swallowed up in life. Thus alone can God become all in all. the sovereign of the universe. Finite evil, if it ends in infinite good, ceases to be evil; for the finite, compared with the infinite, is nothing. But, if finite evil ends in eternal evil, then evil reigns by the side of good, sharing the universe; and God can never be the All-in-All. But Jesus and Paul have taught us that all men are to be drawn to Christ, and all are to be made alive in him. When this final consummation arrives, then all doubts will be answered, difficulties explained, problems solved, and partial evil be seen as universal good.

And now, if you ask, "What do we know about the other life?" we must reply that we know very little about it. It is evident that we are not intended to know much. Perhaps it would take our thoughts too far away from our duties here. *This* is our sphere while we remain in it. If we were able to look into the great world beyond, we might repine at being obliged to remain in this so long. Just as God has placed great gulfs of space between the planets, so that the inhabitants of each shall only know the affairs of its own globe, he has placed a gulf between this world and the future life. Thus, he makes it our duty to think, not of dying, but of living; not of the hereafter, but of the here; not of the world to come, but of the world that is. Every day we are to prepare, not for death, but for life; for, if we live well and wisely here, we may certainly trust God as to our hereafter.

This, however, I think we may say, that death, when it comes, must be considered not a bad thing, but a good thing. Since the Almighty sends death to every one of his creatures to whom he has given life, since death is as universal as life, death must be a blessing as well as life. It is a part of the same scheme, it is a step forward, only another phase of living. Some great advantage must be connected with this event which we call death. It is made fearful when we look forward to it from a distance, that we may not too rashly seek it, before we have had enough of the discipline of this world. But when it comes it usually is welcome; and it may be that, when we look back upon it from the other world, we shall smile to think that we should ever have been afraid of it.

This also we know of the other world: That it is created by the same Being who has made this world; it is another mansion in the house of our Father. Consider, then, what he has done for us here, if you wish to know what he will do for us there. If there is infinite variety in this world, — day and night, sleep and waking, changing seasons. flowers and trees, lakes and rivers, mountains and plains, — a vast flora and fauna, — then there will. no doubt, be an equal or a greater variety there ; for surely the Creator has not exhausted himself in making this world. There, as here, there will be beauty for the eye and ear ; problems for the intellect to investigate ; work to do. full of utility ; society, intercourse, affection ; the power of progress, the sight of goodness and greatness above us to aspire to and reverence. There will be enough to know, enough to do, and enough to love. Perhaps we shall enter more into the interior life of nature, understand more of its mysteries, and come nearer to the working of the creative power whose plastic force flows through all things.

The conception of heaven which has prevailed, as a paradise of delight. a garden of all enjoyments, is not likely to be realized. Such a heaven as this would soon become tiresome. Passive enjoyment is not what God intends for us. He educates us here by stern necessity to toil ; he teaches us caution, prudence. industry, by a sharp discipline : and it is probable that something of this kind of education may be continued hereafter. One of the great blessings of this present life is the sense of progress, of improvement. And as we are told that "hope abides," as well as faith and love, there will be always before us some new vision of beauty, truth, and love to which to aspire. There, as here, heaven will greatly consist in forgetting the things behind and reaching out to those that are before; in perpetual ascent toward the Great Source of all being. There is only one place in the New Testament where any thing is told us concerning the mode of existence hereafter, and that is by Paul in his chapter on the resurrection. In that wonderful passage, where he seems to pass the flaming bounds of space and time; after assuring us that redemption will be coextensive with sin, he goes on to describe the end, when Jesus, having subdued all evil, shall give up the kingdom to the Father, to whom he himself shall be subject and subordinate. He lifts, for a moment, the corner of the veil which hangs between this life and the next, and allows us a glimpse into those diviner mansions of our Father's great building, the universe. He goes on to unfold what was before secret, and thus virtually gives us a new revelation in regard to the future life. There will be bodies, he says, there as here, only of a higher kind than these, — more spiritual, more powerful, more glorious, incorruptible. Those bodies will possess faculties to us now unknown. They will furnish means to the soul of much keener penetration into nature, fuller communication with other minds, and far nobler intercourse with the angelic societies. And this is what we might expect. All is progress here. Every year brings us some new invention. We can now converse with friends across the Atlantic, call on the sun to paint portraits and landscapes, and with a little prism of glass find out the chemistry of the sun and the stars. A few years ago all this would be regarded as an impossibility or as a miracle. In a future life, we may expect to find far greater manifestations of the power of the advancing soul to use the laws of the universe for its ends, and to penetrate mysteries of being stranger than any thing hitherto known. The great law of all existence is progress, — progress accelerated as we ascend nearer to God. Knowledge shall pass away, resolved into higher knowledge. Earthly interests, which now seem so vast, will by and by appear as the toys of childhood. We shall look back from a higher world on our present civilization, and on our present Christianity, as we now look back on the monstrous strife and perturbation of past geologic ages. We may seem to ourselves hereafter as the Saurians and Trilobites seem to us now. But through all change. within all progress, something will for ever abide. *Faith* will abide. We shall carry with us into all worlds the same essential trust in the Infinite love which sustains us now. *Hope* will abide. For, whatever heights of being we may ascend, whatever depths of experience we may explore. there will ever open before us new vistas of knowledge, activity, and joy. And *love* will abide. — the same. but better. Love, uniting us with God and all his creatures. lifting us into communion with all goodness in all worlds; love making us, and keeping us, at one with God for ever and for ever.

> "And so, beside the silent sea,
> I wait the muffled oar;
> No harm from him can come to me,
> On ocean or on shore."

www.ingramcontent.com/pod-product-compliance
Lightning Source LLC
Chambersburg PA
CBHW022124160426
43197CB00009B/1145